THE BOY FROM CLEARWATER

清水

THE BOY FROM CLEARWATER

YU PEI-YUN · ZHOU JIAN-XIN

TRANSLATION BY LIN KING

Montclair | Amsterdam | Hoboken

This is an Em Querido book
Published by Levine Querido

LEVINE QUERIDO
Levine Querido
www.levinequerido.com • info@levinequerido.com

Levine Querido is distributed by Chronicle Books

Text copyright © 2023 by Yu Pei-Yun
Illustration copyright © 2023 by Zhou Jian-Xin
Translation copyright © 2023 by Lin King

All rights reserved

Library of Congress Control Number: 2023931856

Hardcover ISBN 978-1-64614-279-8
Paperback ISBN 978-1-64614-280-4

Printed in India

Published October 2023
First Printing

The text type was set in Sequentialist BB.

COLOR KEY FOR SPOKEN LANGUAGES

To highlight the diversity of languages in Taiwan during this time period—including Hoklo Taiwanese, Mandarin Chinese, and Japanese—the color-coding system below is used to show which language the characters are speaking.

The pink tones correspond to Part 1, while Part 2 is coded in blue tones.

HOKLO TAIWANESE

ENGLISH

PART 1

MANDARIN CHINESE

JAPANESE

PART 2

MANDARIN CHINESE

JAPANESE

NOTE FROM THE TRANSLATOR

The three main languages used in these books—Taiwanese Hoklo, Mandarin Chinese, and Japanese—all share similar written characters with very different pronunciations and romanization systems. The town 清水, for example, is pronounced "Tshing-tsui" in Taiwanese, "Chingshui" in Mandarin, and "Kiyomizu" in Japanese, all of which mean "clear water," hence the translation of the title *The Boy from Clearwater*.

Accordingly, some characters have names in multiple languages throughout the story. The main character, 蔡焜霖, is referred to by both his Taiwanese name, Tshua Khun-lim, and his Mandarin name, Tsai Kun-lin. Throughout the book, Mandarin is not necessarily romanized using the now-common pinyin system, but also the Wade-Giles and other systems befitting the time periods and regions.

PART 1
THE BOY WHO LOVES TO READ

In 1895, the Qing dynasty of China ceded control of Taiwan and Penghu to the Empire of Japan in the Treaty of Shimonoseki. Japan governed Taiwan for fifty years, until the end of World War II in 1945. The subject of this book, whose name is Tsai Kun-lin in Mandarin Chinese pronunciation and Tshua Khun-lim in Taiwanese Hoklo pronunciation, was born in December 1930 under Japanese rule. The town where he was born was known as Kiyomizu, in Taichu Prefecture, under the Japanese, and is now known as Chingshui in Taichung City.

The area was originally known as Gomach, named by the Taiwanese indigenous Papora people. Later, the Japanese renamed the town Kiyomizu, after the spring that supplies water for the region, on nearby Aofong Hill. The present-day Mandarin Chinese name Chingshui shares the same written characters as the Japanese, and the name means "clear water" in both languages.

Khun-lim's ancestors had tested into the merit-based gentry during the Qing dynasty. His father, Tshua Mi-hong, had received education in Mandarin Chinese and owned a department store. His mother, Lua Uat-kiao, hailed from a wealthy family in present-day Beitun District, Taichung City.

Khun-lim was the eighth of ten siblings. He had three older brothers, four older sisters, and two younger brothers. His sisters, aside from the eldest, Khiong-tsu, grew up in the homes of extended family and friends.

Khun-lim's fifth- and sixth-grade teacher was known by his Japanese name, Kiyomizu Akihiko, as well as by his Mandarin name, Yang Ming-fa, and his Taiwanese name, Iunn Bing-huat. His wife, Loo Soo-tsing, was Khun-lim's kindergarten teacher. Their son, known by his Japanese name, Michio, was classmates with Khun-lim from elementary school through the end of high school; their daughter, known by her Japanese name, Kimiko, attended kindergarten with Khun-lim and would go on to play a significant role in his life.

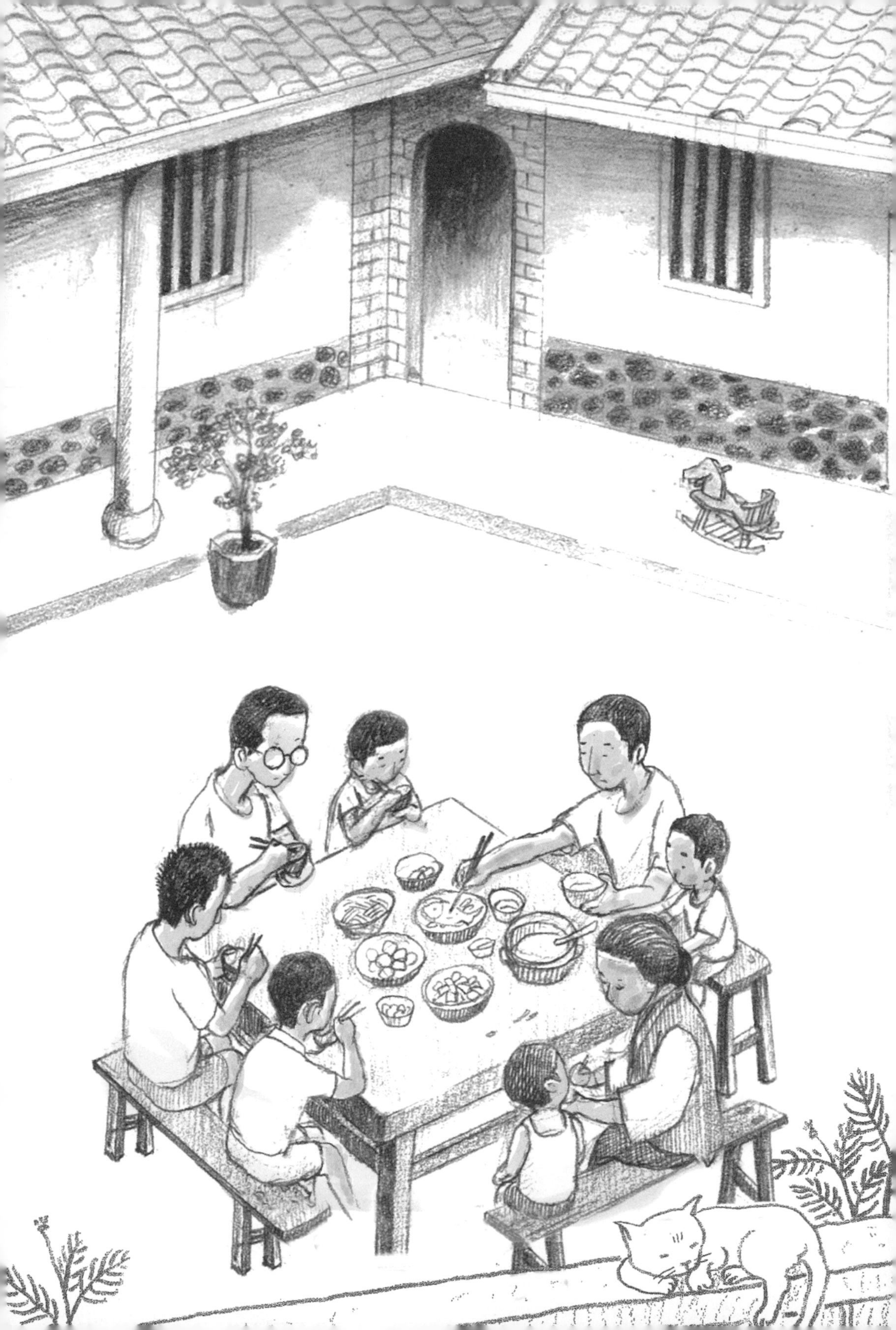

April 21, 1935. Aofong Hill. Dawn.

KHUN-LIM, WATCH YOUR STEP.

?
EARTHQUAKE!
SMASH!

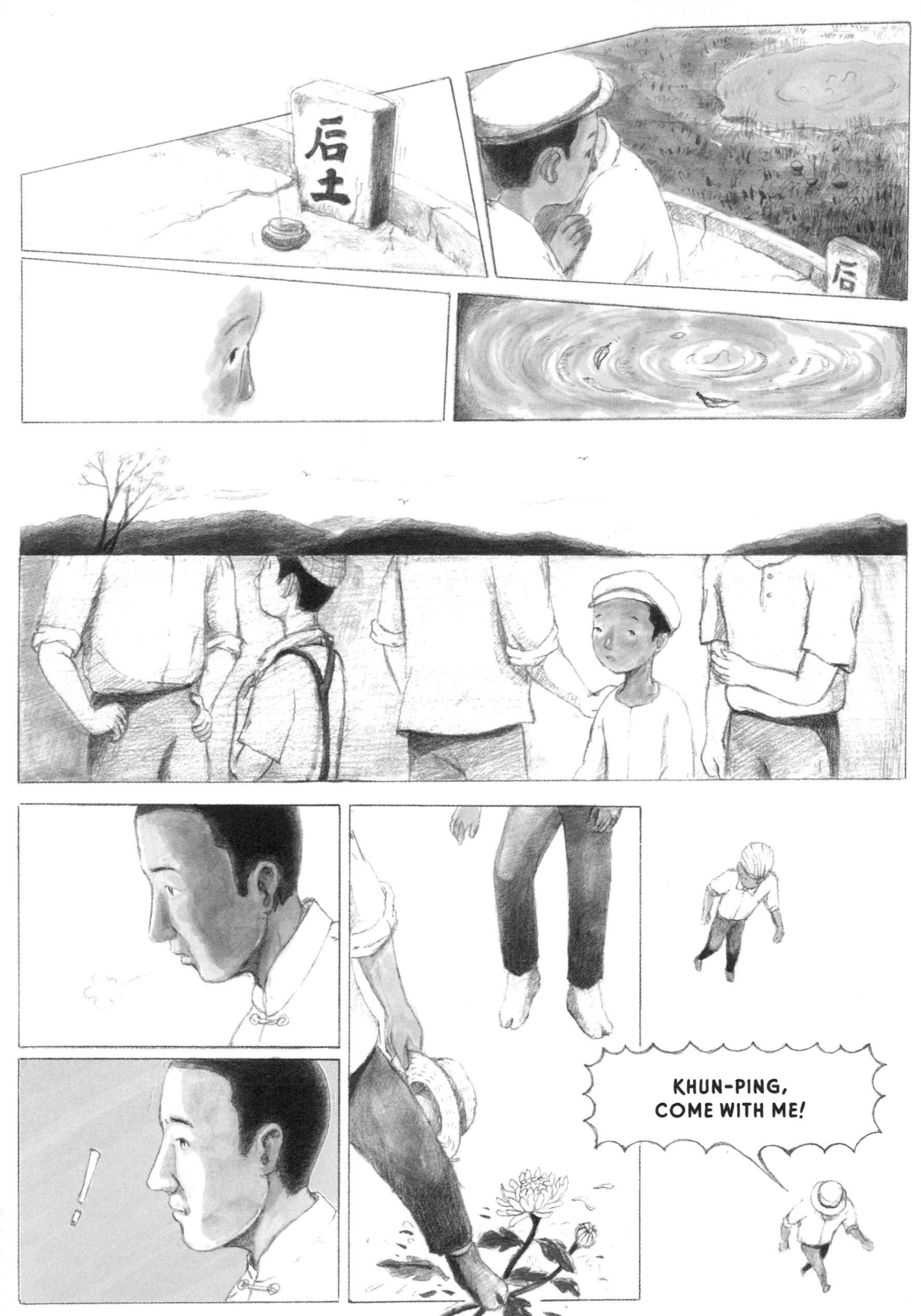
后土
后
!
KHUN-PING,
COME WITH ME!

KHUN-SIU, WATCH THE LITTLE ONES.
I WILL.
BROTHER, DO YOU THINK EVERYTHING'S OKAY AT HOME?
LET'S CLEAN UP AND HURRY DOWN.
HERE, BE CAREFUL WITH THIS.
OKAY.
I WANT TO HELP TOO.
YOU HOLD THE TURTLE CAKE, THEN.

KHUN-TSAN, LOOK AFTER KHUN-LIM.

WATCH YOUR STEP.

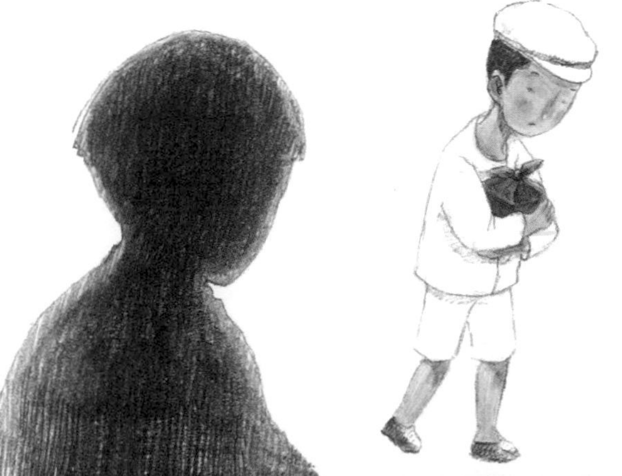

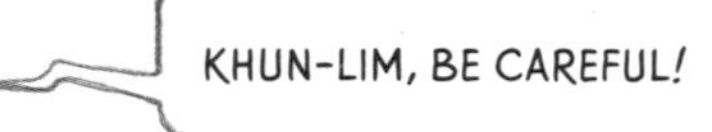
KHUN-LIM, BE CAREFUL!

The sudden earthquake devastated the Dunzijiao region (present-day Houli District in Taichung City) and Kiyomizu Town (present-day Chingshui District). Its impact was felt all over Taiwan, killing or injuring over 15,000 people and collapsing over 60,000 buildings.

Tshua Khun-lim, born December 1930, was only four years old at the time. The Tshua home was severely damaged by the earthquake.

THERE ARE SO MANY INJURED PEOPLE ON THE STREETS. POOR THINGS.
KHIONG-TSU.
MM?
GO GIVE RICE TO PEOPLE WHO NEED IT.
WANT TO COME HELP ME?
YES!

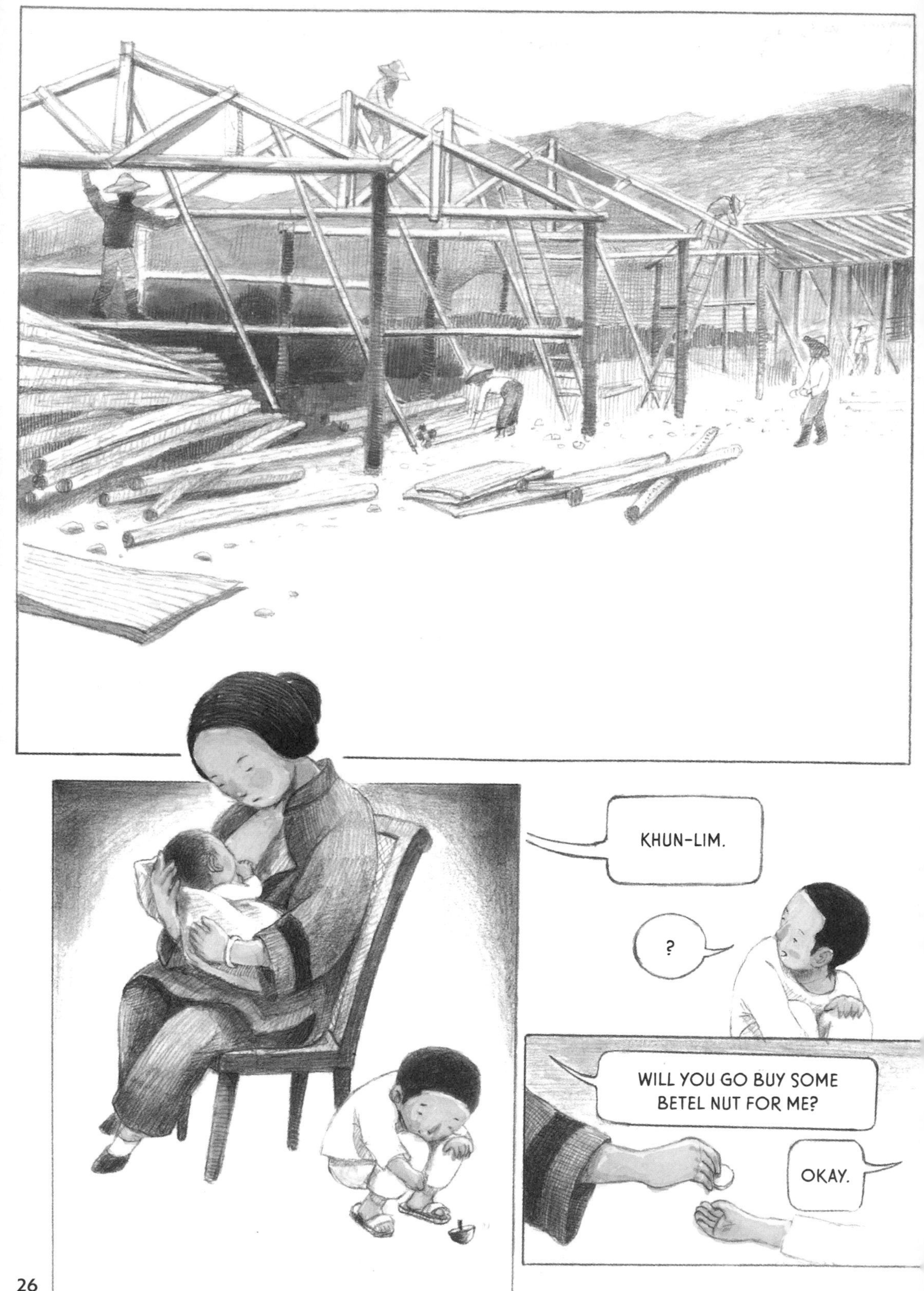
KHUN-LIM.
?
WILL YOU GO BUY SOME BETEL NUT FOR ME?
OKAY.

It was Khun-lim's first time venturing out alone at night.

The Tshua home was fully restored by the end of 1935.

KHIONG-TSU!

OKAY, RIGHT AWAY.

TAKE KHUN-LIM TO THE STORE
FOR A SET OF NEW CLOTHES.

KHUN-LIM, LET'S GO SEE BA.

OKAY!

Eighteenth Kham, Kiyomizu Town.

KHIONG-TSU, CONGRATULATIONS ON THE ENGAGEMENT!
THANK YOU. YOU, AH-SIU, AND BI-KHIM MUST COME TO THE WEDDING!
WE ARE! WE'VE PLANNED IT ALL OUT.
IF IT ISN'T KHUN-LIM!
AH-HONG!
WHERE ARE YOU HEADED?
MMHNGAHNLUNH . . .

梅芳百貨
BA!

WHO BROUGHT YOU HERE?

BA.

MA SAID TO PICK OUT A NEW SET OF CLOTHES FOR KHUN-LIM.

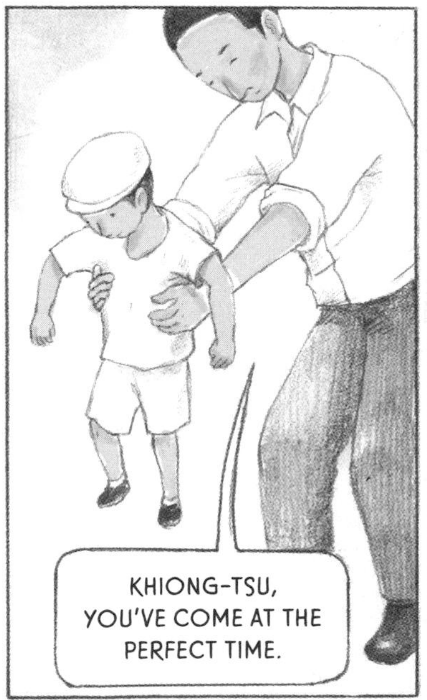
KHIONG-TSU, YOU'VE COME AT THE PERFECT TIME.

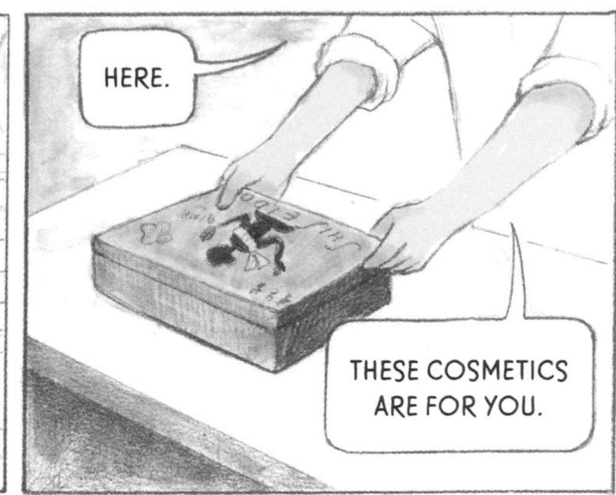
HERE.
THESE COSMETICS ARE FOR YOU.

THANK YOU, BA.

KHUN-PING.
PICK OUT A SAILOR SUIT WITH KHUN-LIM.

OKAY.

COME.

VERY HANDSOME.

CRACKLE
CRACKLE

HURRY, KHUN-LIM,
GO PICK IT UP.

. . .

MA!

MA!

MA!

YOUR SISTER AND BROTHER-IN-LAW ARE COMING OVER TODAY. YOU'LL HAVE TO BE GOOD!

OKAY.

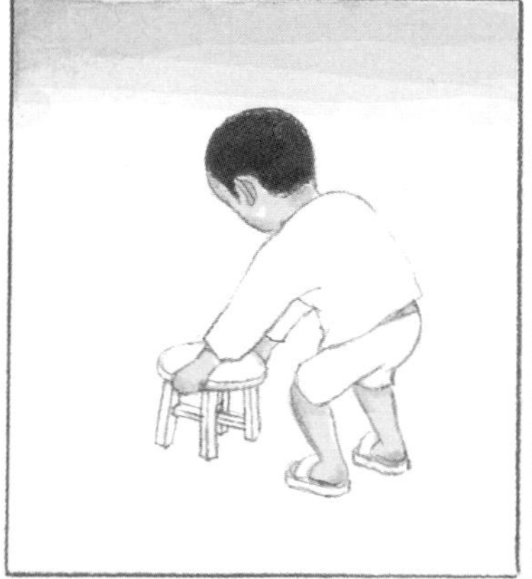

THEY'RE HERE!
SISTER!

Five-year-old Khun-lim was distraught over the marriage of the sister who cared for and pampered him. This was his first small taste of bereavement.

October 1936. Kiyomizu Kindergarten.

WAIT FOR ME.
?
WHAT'S THAT?
A TRAIN!
I WANT TO PLAY TOO.
SURE.
HOW PRETTY.
GOOD MORNING, MS. LOO!

DING!
DING!
DING!
TIME FOR CLASS, EVERYBODY!

IF WE HOLD HANDS AND HEAD TO THE MEADOW,

WE'LL ALL TURN INTO SWEET LITTLE BIRDS.

WE'LL SING TOGETHER, OUR SHOES TAP-TAPPING,

UNDER THE CLEAR SKY, OUR SHOES TAP-TAPPING.

"Shoes Tap-Tapping," Lyrics: Kiyomizu Katsura.
Music: Hirota Ryutaro. A nursery rhyme released in 1936.

*Kiyomizu Kimiko is the Japanese name of Iunn Pik-ju, the daughter of Khun-lim's kindergarten teacher, Loo Soo-tsing. It was common in Taiwan for people to adopt Japanese names during the "Japanization" movement at this time.

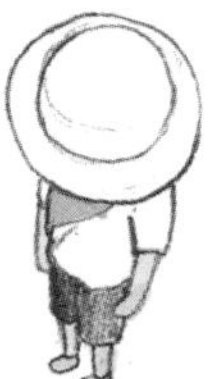

IF WE HOLD HANDS AND HEAD TO THE MEADOW
WE'LL ALL TURN INTO SWEET LITTLE BIRDS
UNDER THE CLEAR SKY, OUR SHOES TAP-TAPPING
WE'LL SING TOGETHER, OUR SHOES TAP-TAPPING

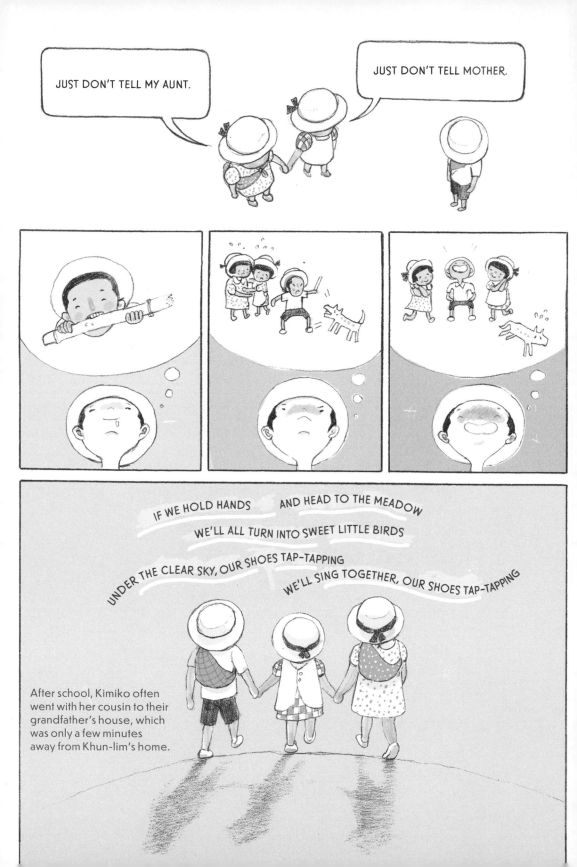

After school, Kimiko often went with her cousin to their grandfather's house, which was only a few minutes away from Khun-lim's home.

SNAP!

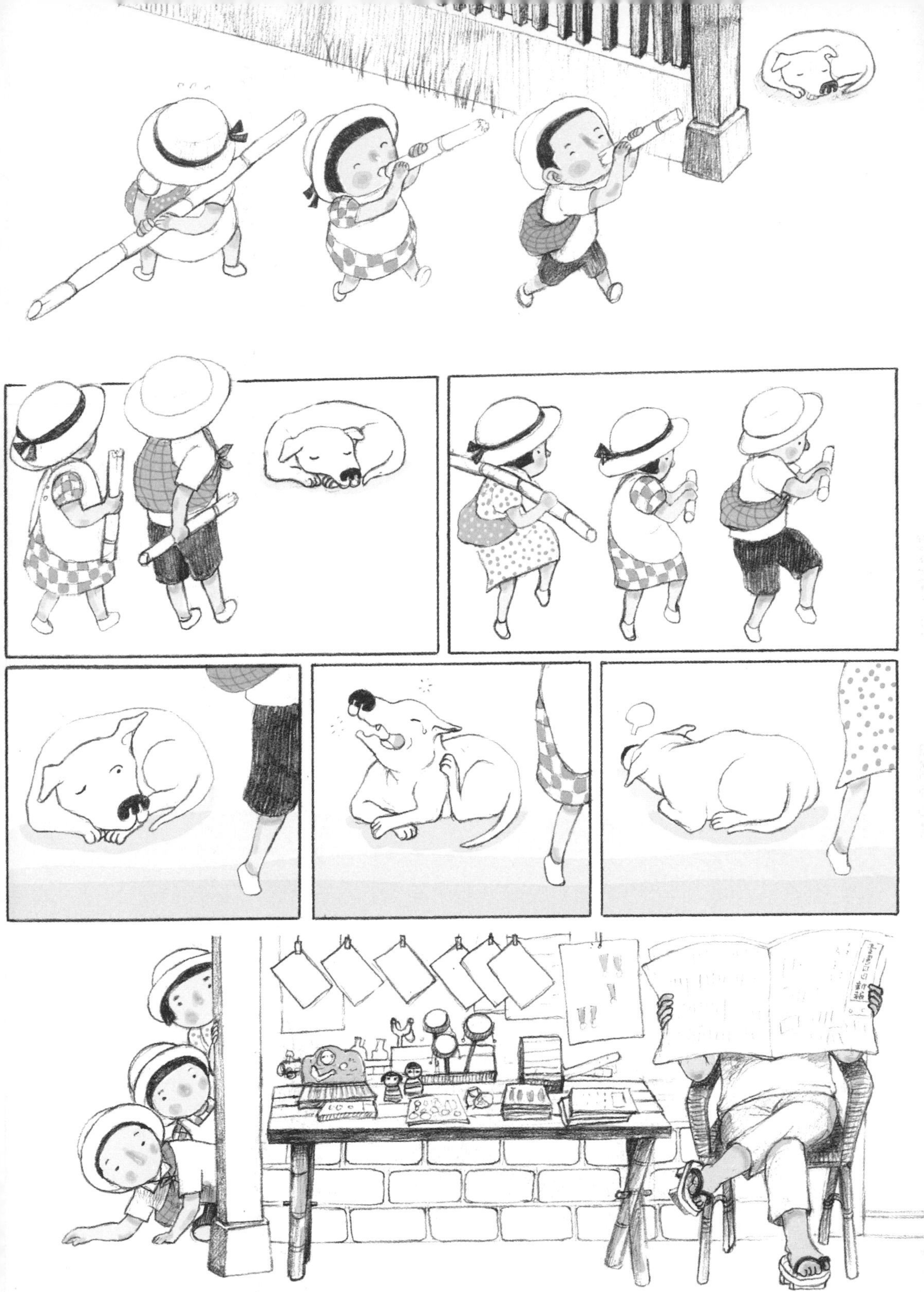

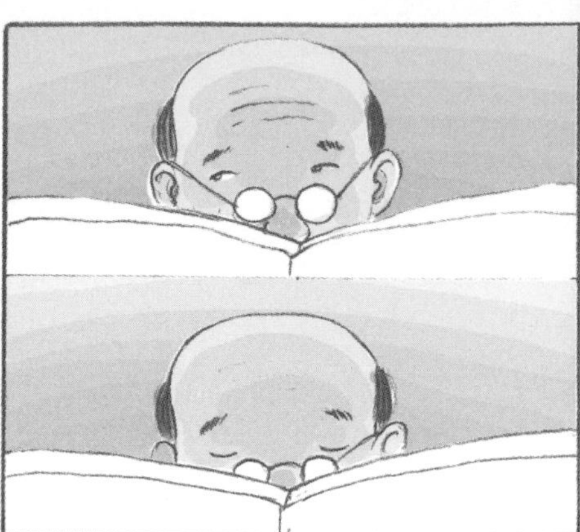

GOODBYE.
BYE.

MORNING.
GOOD MORNING, MS. LOO.
GOOD MORNING.
...
?
KHUN-LIM, COME WITH ME.

It was Khun-lim's first great adventure alone in the company of girls. Despite being scolded by a beloved teacher, he would go on to consider it the most unforgettably bittersweet memory of his childhood.

December 1937. Kiyomizu Public School.

GOOD MORNING, PRINCIPAL KAWAMURA.
MORNING.
KHUN-LIM, I'LL COME MEET YOU IN YOUR CLASSROOM AFTER SCHOOL.
OKAY.

"Red Dragonflies." Lyrics: Miki Rofu. Music: Yamada Kosaku.

Door sign: Principal's Office

THE RED DRAGONFLIES IN THE RED SUNSET . . .

YOU SING IT SO OFTEN, BUT DO YOU KNOW WHAT YOU'RE SINGING?

NOPE!

IT'S TALKING ABOUT DRAGONFLIES IN THE SUNSET. *TONBO* MEANS DRAGONFLY.

I SEE!
COME, I WANNA SHOW YOU SOMETHING.

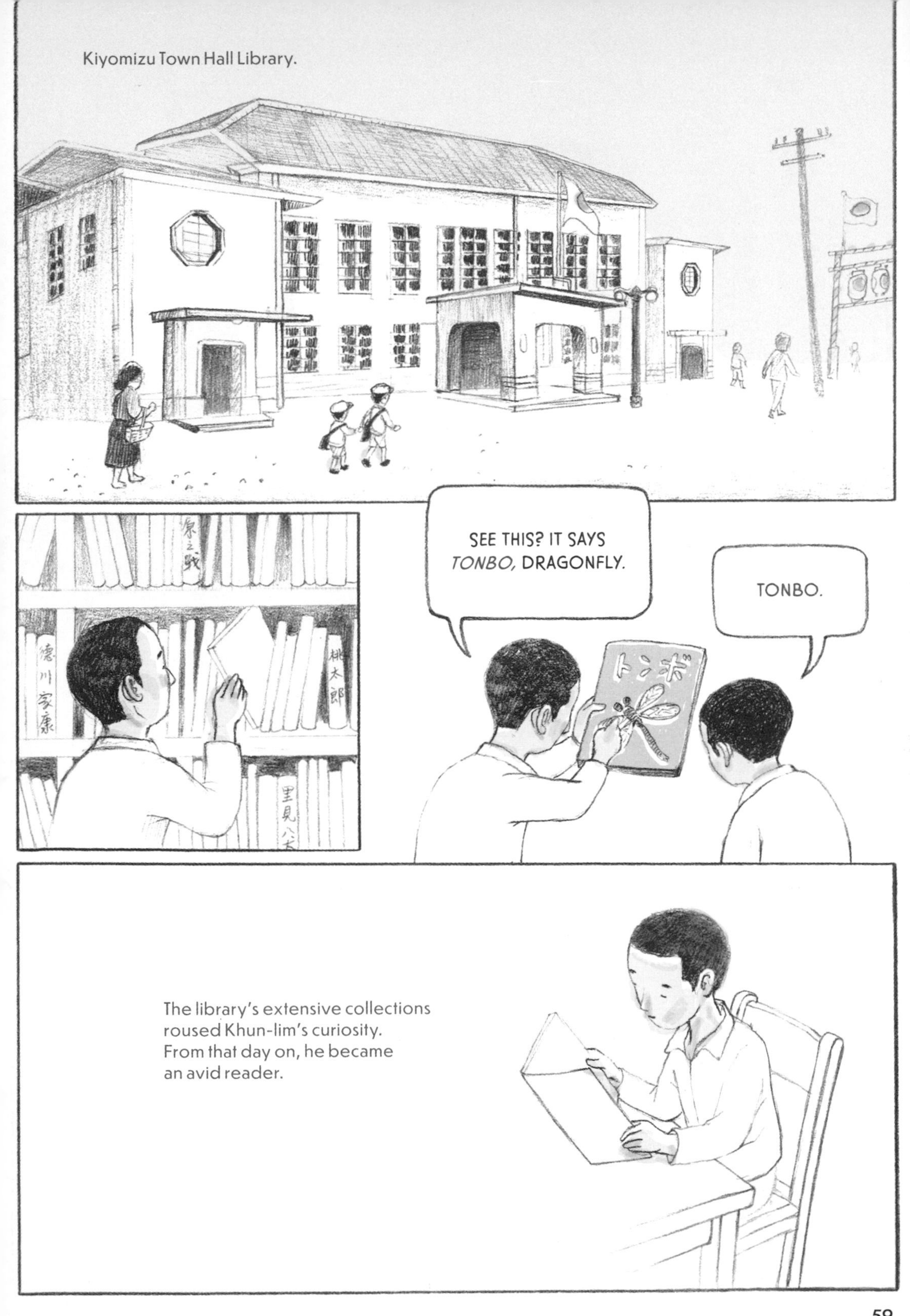
Kiyomizu Town Hall Library.
徳川家康
桃太郎
SEE THIS? IT SAYS *TONBO,* DRAGONFLY.
トンボ
TONBO.
The library's extensive collections roused Khun-lim's curiosity. From that day on, he became an avid reader.

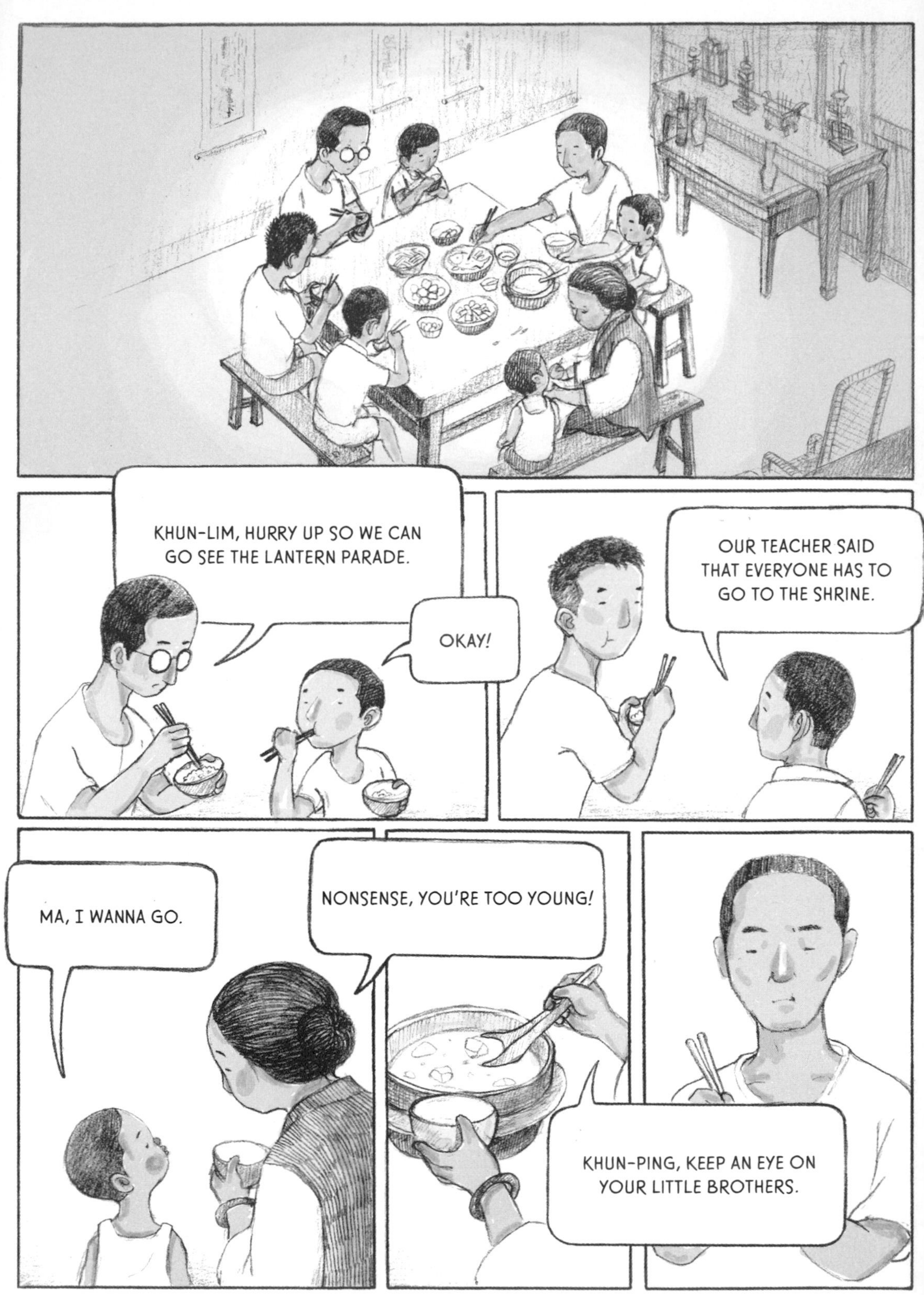
KHUN-LIM, HURRY UP SO WE CAN GO SEE THE LANTERN PARADE.
OKAY!
OUR TEACHER SAID THAT EVERYONE HAS TO GO TO THE SHRINE.
MA, I WANNA GO.
NONSENSE, YOU'RE TOO YOUNG!
KHUN-PING, KEEP AN EYE ON YOUR LITTLE BROTHERS.

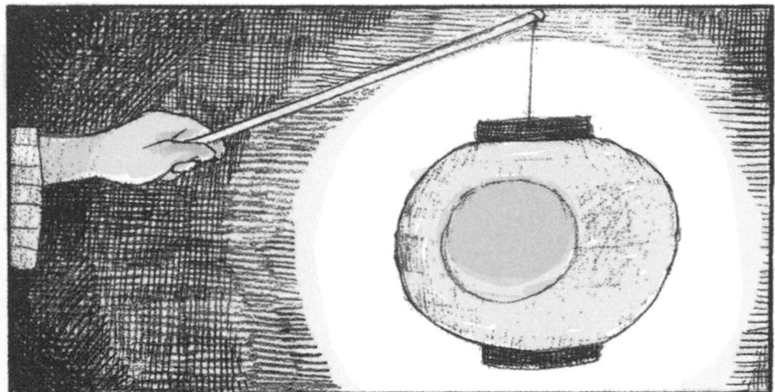

Banner: Victory to the Imperial Army

On December 13, 1937, the Imperial Japanese Army occupied Nanjing, China's then-capital.

LOOK! IF THE SUN IS RISING HIGH AND BRIGHT, ABOVE THE EASTERN SEA,
THEN THE PURE ENERGY OF HEAVEN AND EARTH, AND HOPE SPRINGS ACROSS ALL OF JAPAN.
OH! THE GLORIOUS VIEW OF MOUNT FUJI, TOWERING IN THE MORNING CLOUDS.
FLAWLESS AND UNWAVERING IS THE GOLDEN PRIDE OF JAPAN.

"Patriotic March." Lyrics: Morikawa Yukio. Music: Setoguchi Tokichi. A Japanese march released in 1937.

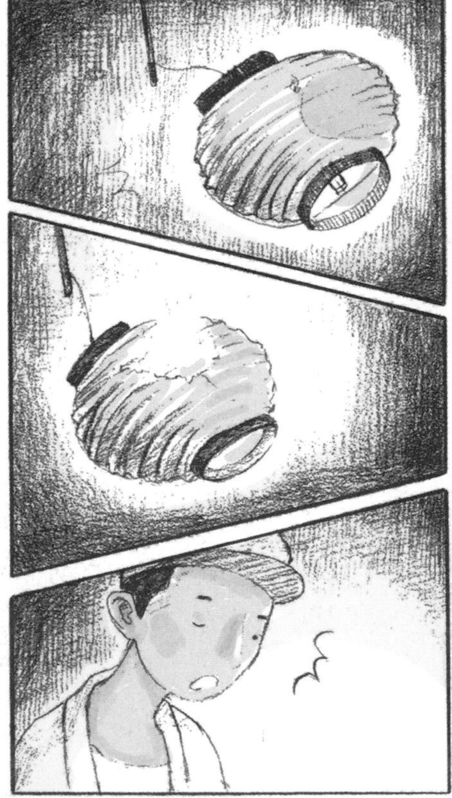

*Lantern parades were a Japanese imperial tradition for celebrating military victories.

That night, safe in his dreams, Khun-lim had no idea that the war was drawing closer and closer to home . . .

In April 1941, Khun-lim started the fifth grade. Due to a change in Japan's educational policy, his school was renamed from Kiyomizu Public School to Kiyomizu Southern National School, and his reassigned homeroom teacher was the notoriously strict Mr. Kiyomizu Akihiko.*

*Kiyomizu Akihiko, also known by his Mandarin name Yang Ming-fa and Taiwanese name Iunn Bing-huat, adopted a Japanese name in accordance with the government's Japanization movement. He was the father of Kimiko, Khun-lim's kindergarten classmate.

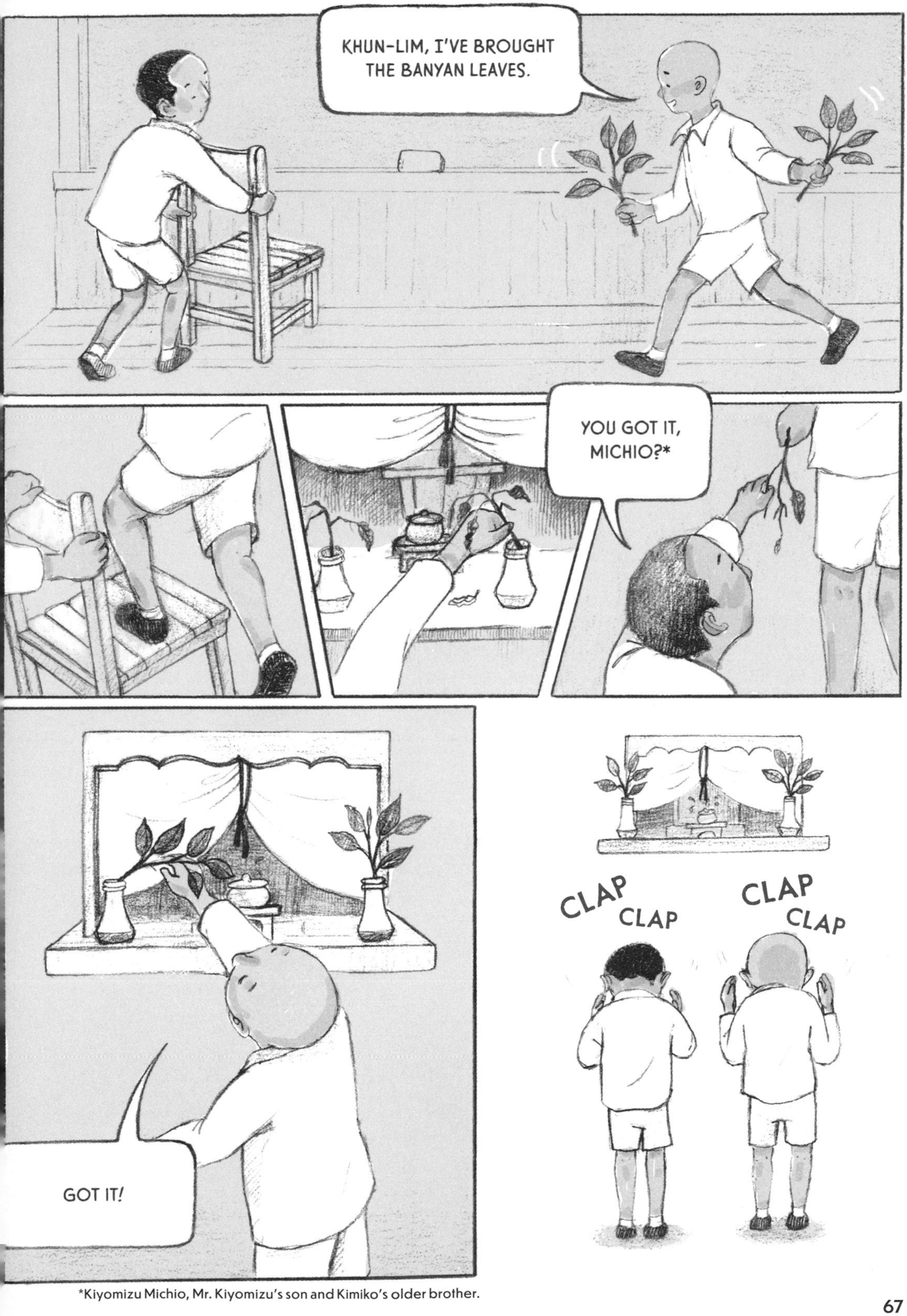

KHUN-LIM, I'VE BROUGHT THE BANYAN LEAVES.

YOU GOT IT, MICHIO?*

*Kiyomizu Michio, Mr. Kiyomizu's son and Kimiko's older brother.

CLASS IS STARTING.
RISE!
ATTENTION!
GOOD MORNING, MR. KIYOMIZU.

HOW MANY OF YOU COMPLETED YOUR HOMEWORK YESTERDAY?
. . .
I HAVE, SIR!
?
KIYOMIZU MICHIO, BRING YOUR HOMEWORK OVER HERE.
. . . YESSIR.

SWISH
SMACK!
WHAT'S THIS? IT'S NOT FINISHED AT ALL!
MR. KIYOMIZU HIT HIS OWN SON . . . !

YOU'RE ALL FIFTH-YEARS NOW. THE ENTRANCE EXAM IS RIGHT AROUND THE CORNER.
WE'LL ALSO BE STUDYING AFTER SCHOOL. YOU'D ALL DO WELL TO STEEL YOURSELVES!
Yessir!
Yessir!
HERE ARE YOUR ESSAYS FROM LAST WEEK.
TSHUA KHUN-LIM!
YESSIR!
VERY WELL WRITTEN!
Thanks to his love of reading, Khun-lim had become an accomplished essay writer, earning Mr. Kiyomizu's encouragement and favor.

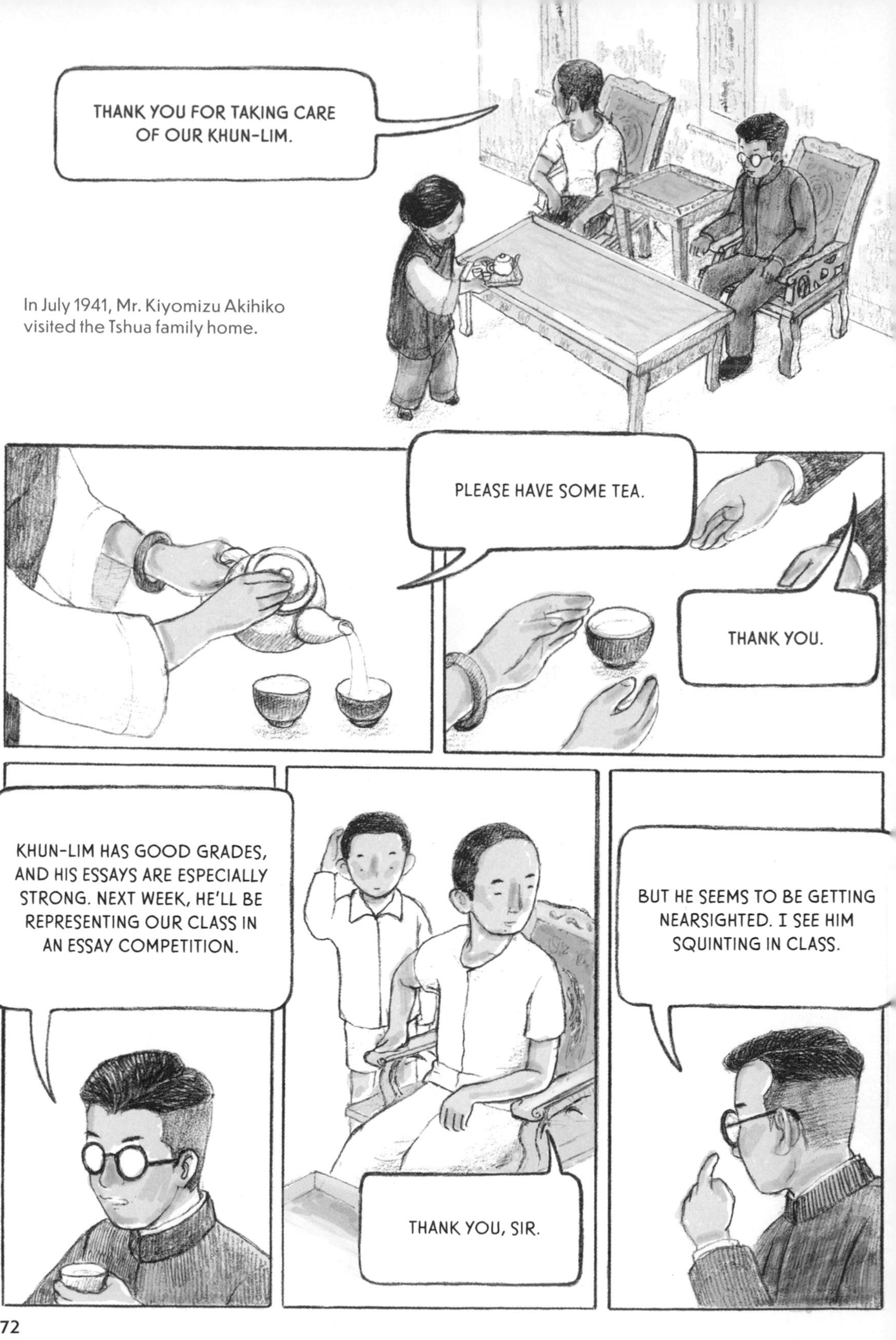

THANK YOU FOR TAKING CARE OF OUR KHUN-LIM.

In July 1941, Mr. Kiyomizu Akihiko visited the Tshua family home.

PLEASE HAVE SOME TEA.

THANK YOU.

KHUN-LIM HAS GOOD GRADES, AND HIS ESSAYS ARE ESPECIALLY STRONG. NEXT WEEK, HE'LL BE REPRESENTING OUR CLASS IN AN ESSAY COMPETITION.
THANK YOU, SIR.
BUT HE SEEMS TO BE GETTING NEARSIGHTED. I SEE HIM SQUINTING IN CLASS.

HE READS TOO MUCH.
YOU'D BETTER HAVE HIS EYES CHECKED.
MR. TSHUA, WHAT PLANS DO YOU HAVE FOR KHUN-LIM'S EDUCATION?
HIS ELDEST AND SECOND-ELDEST BROTHERS BOTH WORK IN MY STORE, AND HIS THIRD-ELDEST BROTHER IS CURRENTLY AT THE SHOKA TRADE SCHOOL. IT'S THE MOST PRACTICAL PATH FOR US BUSINESSPEOPLE.
WITH KHUN-LIM'S PERFORMANCE, HE SHOULD CONTINUE HIS STUDIES. HE OUGHT TO SIT THE TAICHU FIRST SENIOR HIGH SCHOOL EXAM.
TAICHU FIRST? CAN HE REALLY GET IN?

DEFINITELY. HE'S IMPROVED A LOT THIS SEMESTER.

IF MR. KIYOMIZU SAYS SO . . .

. . . THEN WE'LL LET HIM TRY.

KHUN-LIM, LISTEN TO MR. KIYOMIZU AND WORK HARD.

GOODBYE, SIR!

BA SAYS YOU'RE GOING TO TRY FOR TAICHU FIRST.
YEAH, I WANT TO KEEP ON STUDYING.
YOU WANT TO BE A DOCTOR?
I WANT TO BE A TEACHER, LIKE PESTALOZZI.
PESTALOZZI? OH, FROM THAT BOOK YOU'RE READING?
EXACTLY! HE'S AN EDUCATOR FROM SWITZERLAND.

臺中
たいちゅう
TAICHU
祝從軍 
武運長久
滅私奉公

Miyahara Eye Clinic.
宮原眼科醫院
HA! LOOK AT YOU WITH YOUR SCHOLARLY GLASSES.
YOU WEAR THEM TOO!

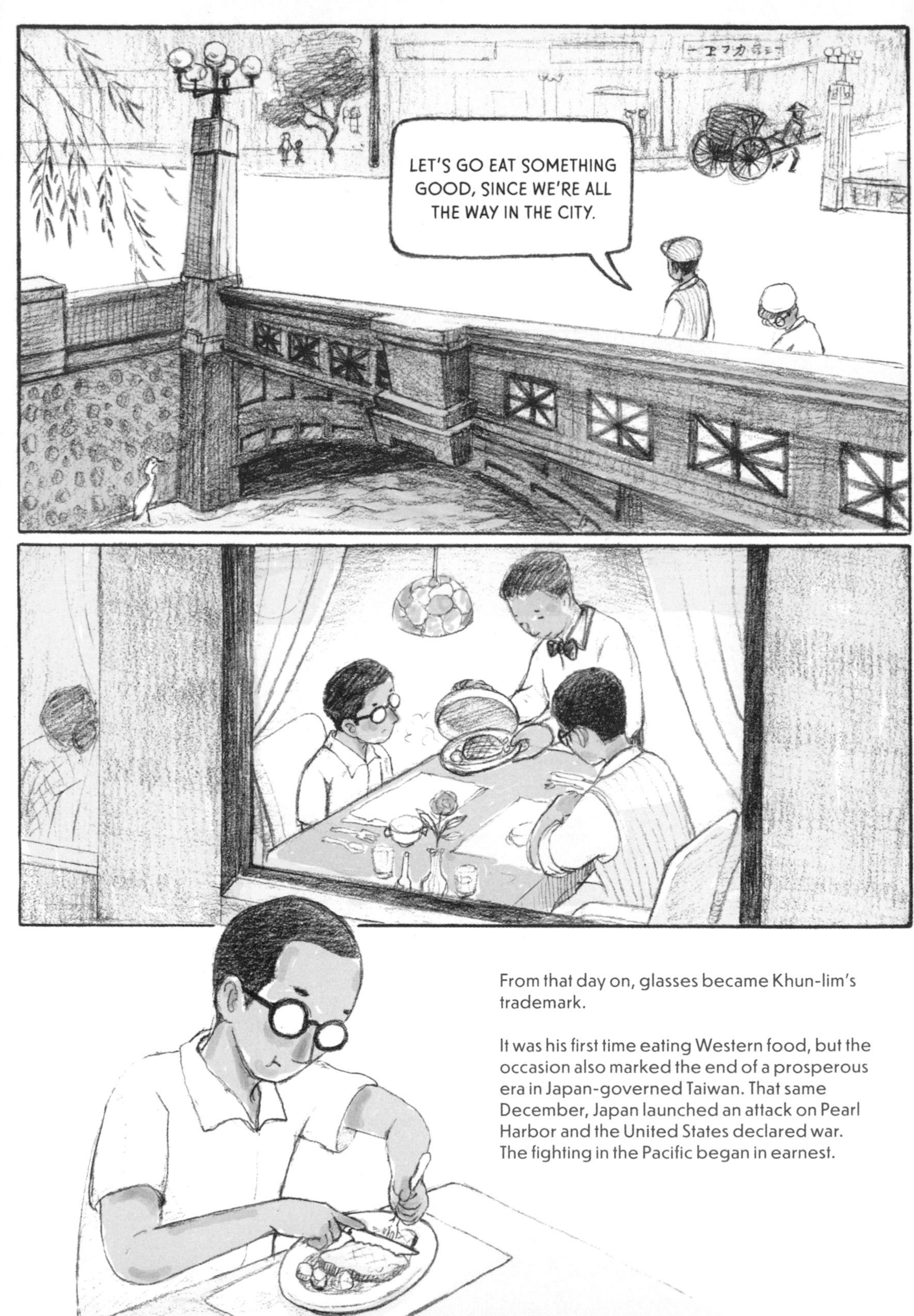
LET'S GO EAT SOMETHING GOOD, SINCE WE'RE ALL THE WAY IN THE CITY.
From that day on, glasses became Khun-lim's trademark.
It was his first time eating Western food, but the occasion also marked the end of a prosperous era in Japan-governed Taiwan. That same December, Japan launched an attack on Pearl Harbor and the United States declared war. The fighting in the Pacific began in earnest.

In March 1943, Khun-lim graduated from Kiyomizu Southern National School and passed the "internal review"* investigations as well as the written portion of the Taichu First entrance exam.

Gate sign: Taichu First Senior High School

*The internal review was a report on a student's grades, attendance, extracurricular activities, and general behavior at school. A teacher provided the initial report, and further investigations were conducted on the student's family and "purity of thought." Only students who passed the "internal review" could proceed with the written and oral exams.

At the oral exam for
Taichu First Senior High School.
DEVOTING HIMSELF TO WORK,
WITHOUT CARE OF FATIGUE OR PAIN,
EXPANDING HIS MIND AFTER
COMPLETING A NIGHT'S LABOR,
LEARNING AND STUDYING,
TIRELESS DESPITE THE
BUSY DAY'S WORK,
NINOMIYA KINJIRO IS THE
EXAMPLE TO WHICH
WE ALL ASPIRE.

VERY WELL SAID.
. . .
NEXT. WHAT SHOULD ONE DO DURING AN AIR RAID?
ONE SHOULD SEEK A SHELTER OR DUGOUT.
IS THIS . . . AN EXAM QUESTION?
Under Mr. Kiyomizu's strict tutelage, both Khun-lim and Mr. Kiyomizu's son, Michio, successfully tested into Taichu First. That year, eight students from Kiyomizu Southern National School passed the exam, an unprecedented high.

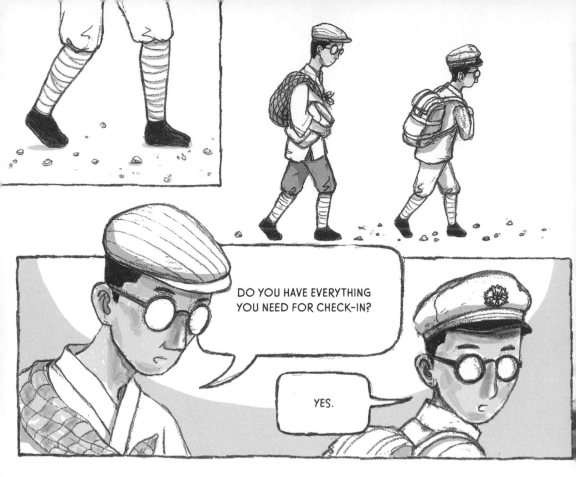

DO YOU HAVE EVERYTHING YOU NEED FOR CHECK-IN?

YES.

Kiyomizu Station.

In April 1943, Khun-lim's eldest brother, Khun-ping, dropped him off on his first day of junior high school.

ntan is a health supplement that was thought of as a cure-all medicine at the time.
e advertising slogan "When traveling, bring Jintan" was widely known.

FRESHMEN, FALL IN!
STAND AT ATTENTION!
WHICH OF YOU CAN SING THE SCHOOL SONG?
YOU DON'T KNOW IT!?
TAKE OFF YOUR GLASSES!
I'VE ONLY JUST ARRIVED, SENPAI.
SMACK!
SMACK!
SMACK!
TSHUA KHUN-LIM! DON'T THINK I DIDN'T NOTICE HOW YOU DIDN'T GREET ME TODAY!
SMACK!
Beginning with his first night in the Taichu First dormitories, Khun-lim was subjected to a rigid seniority system and suffered at the hands of the older boys.

DONG
HAH!
CLACK!
OW!
Students had to undergo military training in addition to their coursework. For self-defense and attacking, they had to choose between judo or kendo in their first year.

Often, for nighttime military training, they would walk for ten or twenty kilometers all at once.
Students were sometimes told to cut grass at airfields or shovel earth on military bases as part of "citizenry service." Their labor made them members of the Imperial Japanese Army.
WE MUST EACH DO OUR PART FOR OUR COUNTRY!

切符売り場
In Khun-lim's second year, the school dormitories were temporarily converted into a military hospital. Khun-lim moved back to Kiyomizu and, to attend school every day, took the coastal train to Shoka (present-day Changhua) before transferring to Taichu.
HEY, SIAO-TSONG.
MORNING, KHUN-LIM!
COMMUTING FOR ONE AND A HALF HOURS IS SO TIRING!
I ENVY MICHIO SO MUCH. I WISH *WE* HAD RELATIVES IN THE CITY TO STAY WITH.
HEY, ISN'T THAT MICHIO'S LITTLE SISTER? SHE GOES TO SHOKA GIRLS' SCHOOL, RIGHT?
HURRY, GO TALK TO HER!
STOP IT . . .
KIMIKO!
?
TSHUA KHUN-LIM HAS SOMETHING TO TELL YOU.

WHAT IS IT?
OH, RIGHT!
YOUR BROTHER SAID TO GIVE YOU THIS. IT'S A LIST OF THINGS HE NEEDS.
THANK YOU.
NO—NO PROBLEM.
NO—NO PROBLEM.
?
THE TRAIN'S HERE!

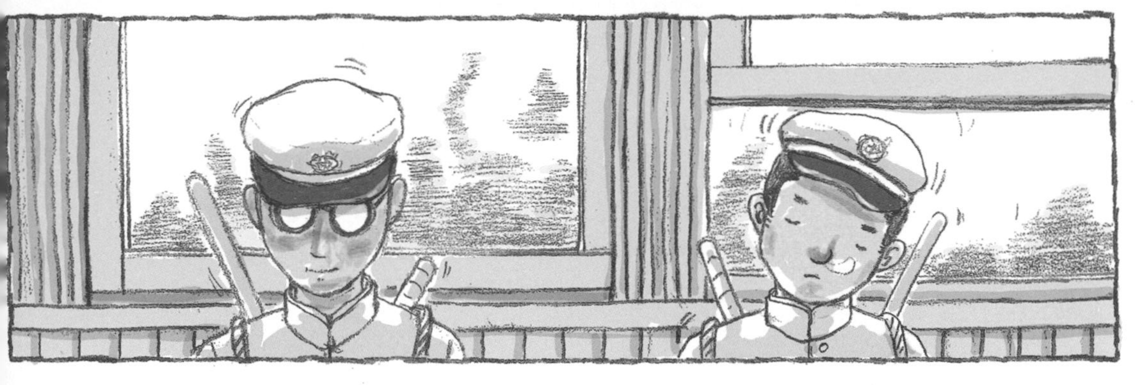

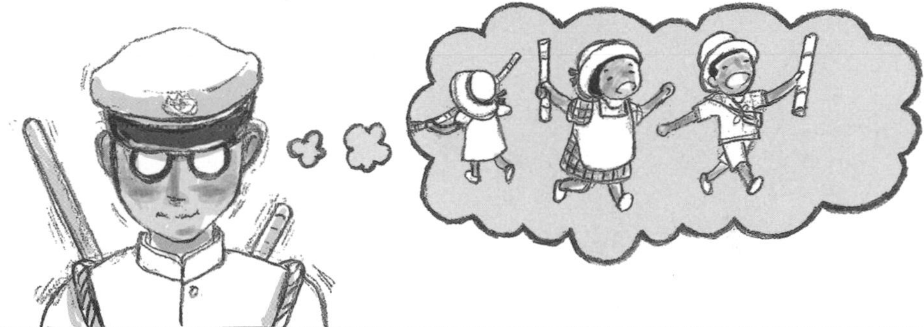

WHEEOOOO

CREAK

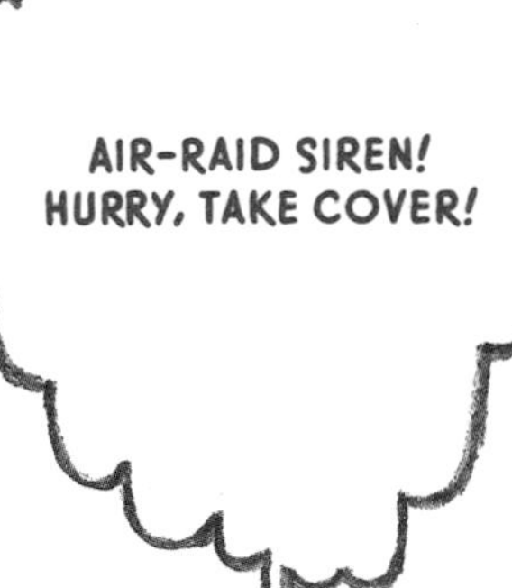
AIR-RAID SIREN!
HURRY, TAKE COVER!

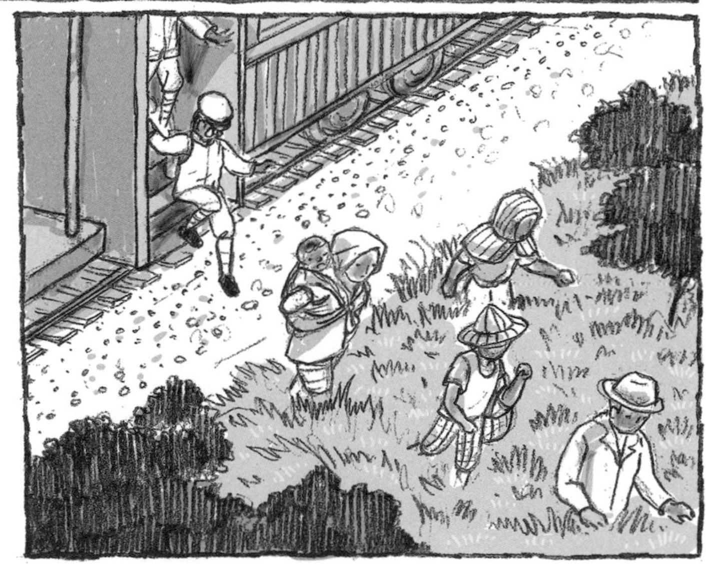

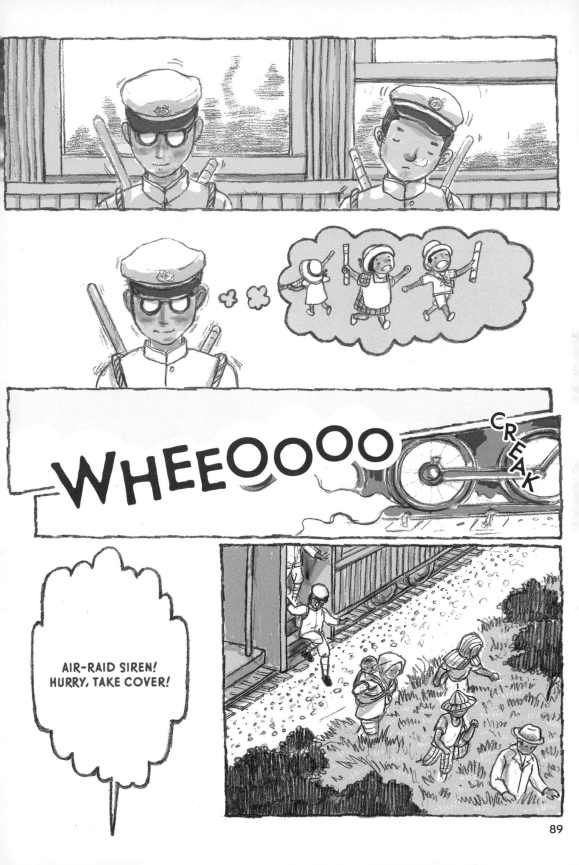

HURRY! WE'RE GOING TO BE LATE!
WHY ARE YOU LATE?! SUCH UNPATRIOTIC BOYS!
BUT WE RISKED OUR LIVES GETTING HERE . . .
WE'RE GOING TO THE MOUNTAIN TODAY.
Surrounded by the sounds of war, Khun-lim nursed his first-ever crush.

January 1945. The Tshua home.

KHUN-TSAN, YOU MUST TAKE GOOD CARE OF YOURSELF.
TAKE THIS AMULET FROM THE TEMPLE.
THE GODS BE WITH YOU.
STAY ON YOUR TOES AND COME HOME SAFE.
I WILL, BA.

YOUR SISTER KHIONG-TSU IS BACK.
GREET YOUR GRANDFATHER AND GRANDMOTHER.
GRANDFATHER, GRANDMOTHER.
LOOK HOW TALL YOU'VE GOTTEN.
GOOD BOY!
SISTER.
SISTER.
THIS IS FOR THE FAMILY.
?
. . .
THANKS. SUGAR IS SO EXPENSIVE THESE DAYS.
BLACK MARKET?

KHUN-TSAN, YOU'RE REALLY SOMETHING!
TESTING INTO THE ARMY AS A JUNIOR PILOT . . .
I HEARD THERE WERE THOUSANDS OF CANDIDATES. IT WAS HARDER THAN GETTING INTO TAIHOKU IMPERIAL UNIVERSITY!
THE TRAINING BASE IS IN NARA, RIGHT?
WHAT KIND OF TIMING IS THIS? HE ONLY JUST PASSED THE TEST, AND HE ALREADY HAS TO GO!
AIGH! EVEN IF HE HADN'T TAKEN THE PILOT TEST, HE WOULD'VE BEEN DRAFTED IN MARCH ANYHOW.
DON'T WORRY, MA, IT'S JUST TRAINING AT THE AVIATION BASE FOR NOW.
WE WON'T BE FIGHTING!
THE PHOTOGRAPHER'S HERE! GET READY, EVERYBODY.

Khun-lim is in the back row, the third from the right.

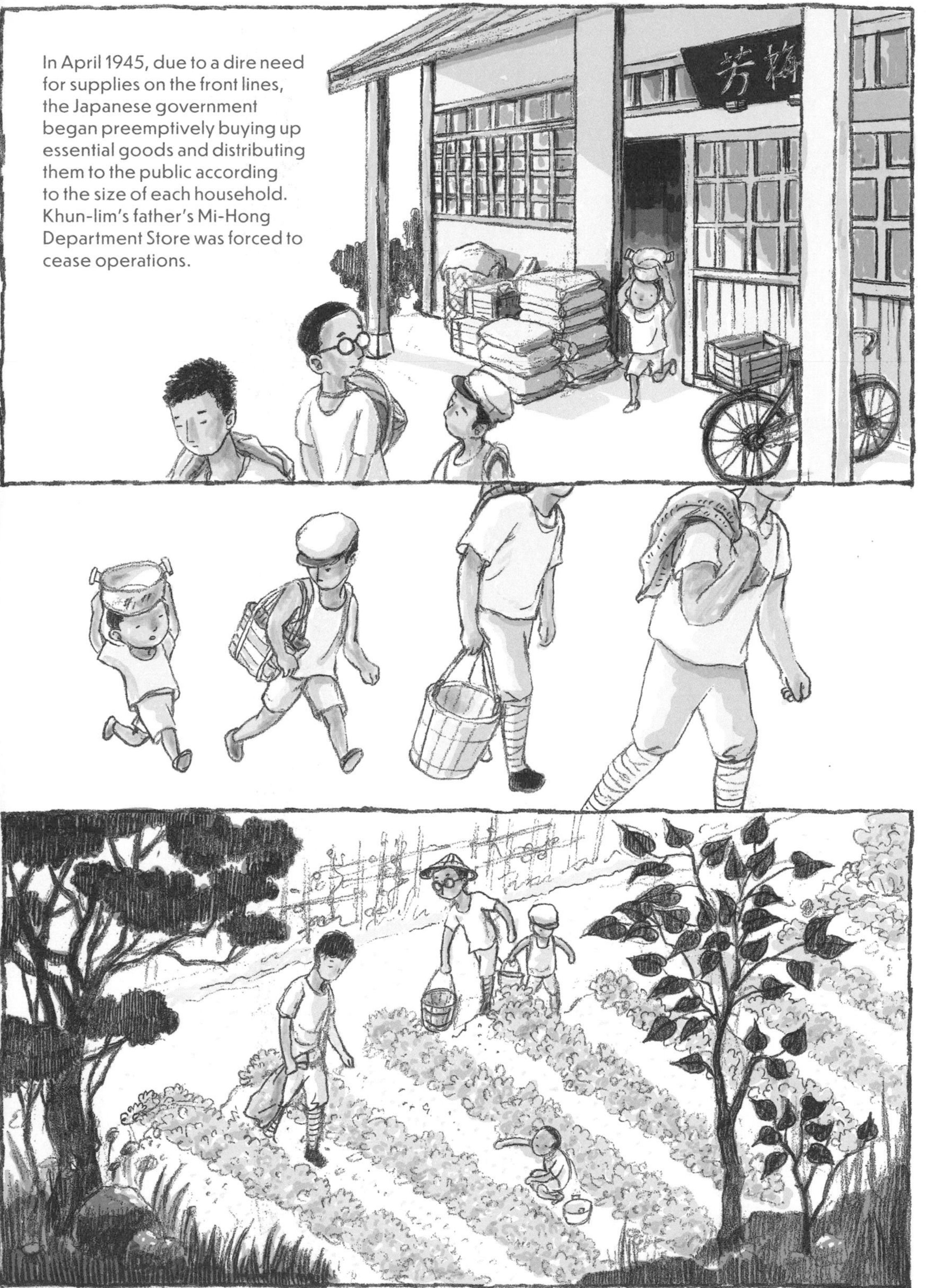
In April 1945, due to a dire need for supplies on the front lines, the Japanese government began preemptively buying up essential goods and distributing them to the public according to the size of each household. Khun-lim's father's Mi-Hong Department Store was forced to cease operations.
梅芳

OKAY.
YOU THREE TAKE THE PEANUTS HOME FIRST.

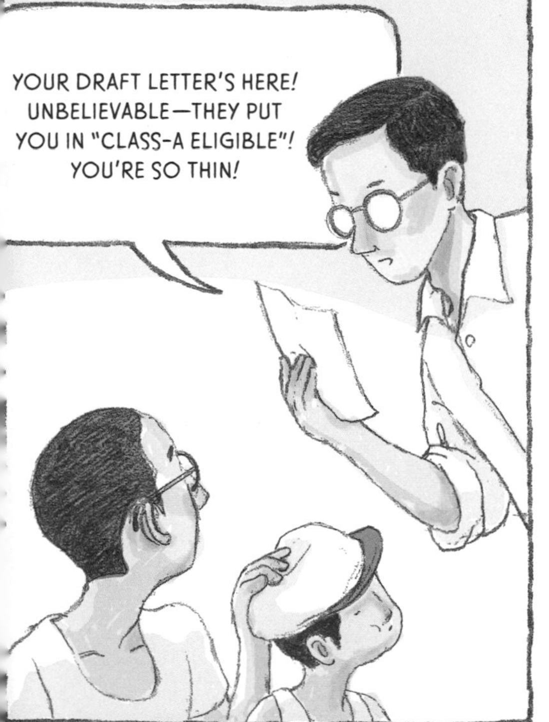

The Cabinet of Japan passed the Prospectus for Wartime Education Measures, which put a pause on all education beyond elementary school.

Khun-lim, who was not yet fifteen, was drafted as a student soldier.

April 1945. The student soldiers of Taichu First were stationed at Kiyomizu Southern National School.

I MUST DO MY BEST FOR THE HOLY WAR!

ACK, CHINESE MEDICINE PORRIDGE AGAIN.
IT'S DISGUSTING!
TSHUA KHUN-LIM!
BROTHER, I'VE GOT PEANUTS!
KHUN-TSIONG!

At the end of April 1945, some students went by truck to defend the arsenals in eastern Taiwan.

Khun-lim's squad, however, went on foot to their assigned post at Shuinan Military Airport.

One dawn in early August 1945. Shuinan Military Airport.

WHEEOOEEOO

WHEEOOO
AGAIN?!
HURRY!

IT'S A B-25!
TCK
TCK
TCK
TCK
TCK
TCK
TCK
TCK
TCK
HURRY!
TCK
TCK
TCK
TCK
I WONDER IF EVERYONE'S OKAY AT HOME . . .

Z
Z
Z

ALL CLEAR!
FALL IN!
THIS MEANS WE ONLY HAVE TO DO HALF THE DRILLS TODAY.

August 15, 1945.
IT'S SO QUIET TODAY.
NO AIR RAIDS ALSO MEANS NO SUGARCANE, THOUGH.
TRUE.
OI, FOCUS!

August 16, 1945.
6:00 a.m.
YESTERDAY . . .
. . . THE HOLY EMPEROR ANNOUNCED THE END OF THE WAR OVER THE RADIO.
HOW COME?
OVER? THE WAR'S OVER?
HOW COULD WE HAVE LOST? IT'S THE HOLY WAR!
DID WE SURRENDER?
BUT WHY?

THE EMPEROR . . .
HOW CAN WE *POSSIBLY* SURRENDER?
. . .
I CAN'T ACCEPT IT.
WHAT NOW?
WE'LL DEFEND TAIWAN! WE'LL FIGHT TO THE END!
FIGHT TO THE DEATH IF YOU WANT, BUT LEAVE THE REST OF US BE. I STILL WANT TO SEE MY BA AND MA . . .

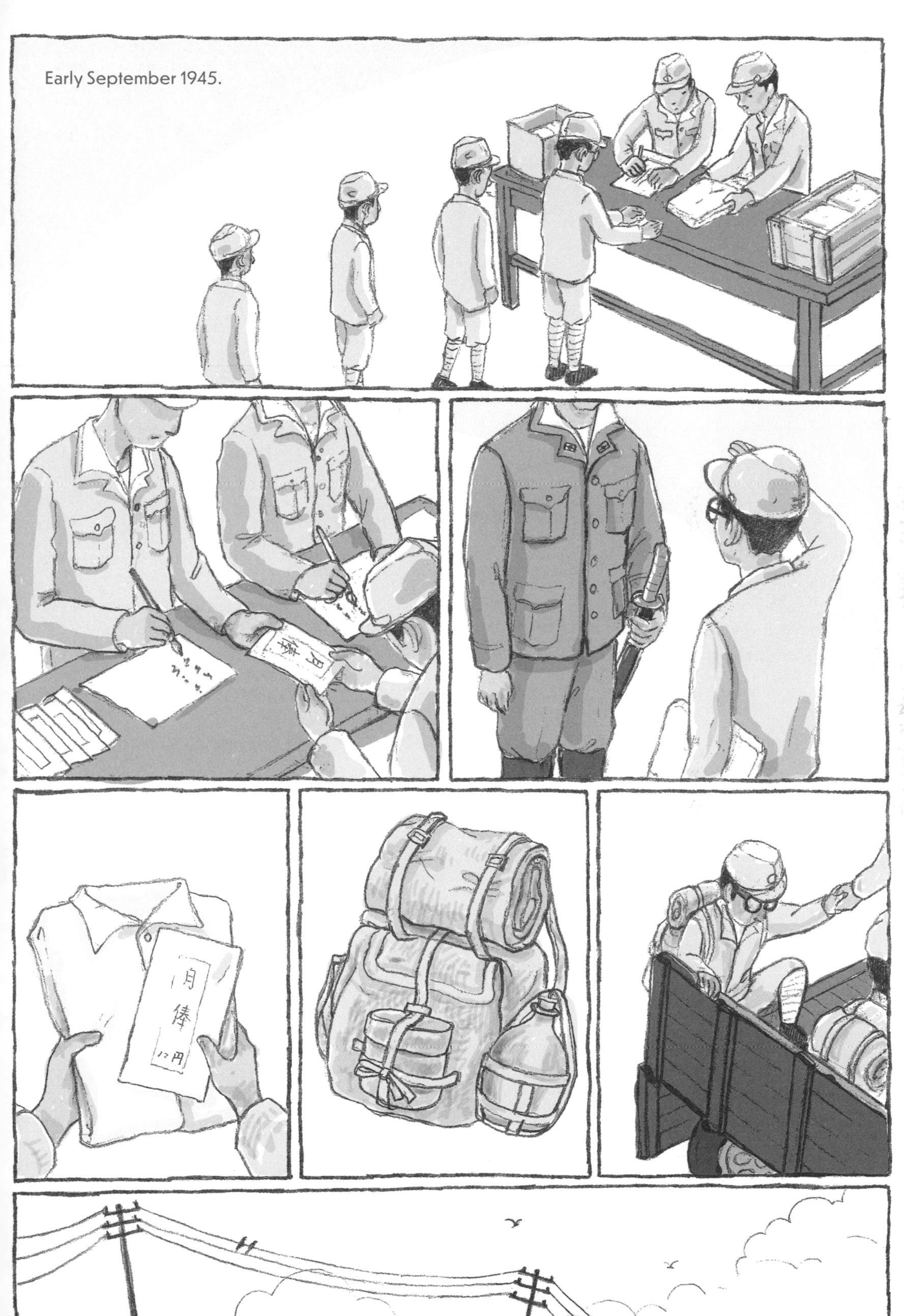
Early September 1945.
月俸
12円

IT'S REALLY
OVER!
BA, MA, I'M COMING HOME!

With nothing but one military shirt and a private's monthly salary of twelve yen in his knapsack, Khun-lim headed home to Kiyomizu.

His days as a soldier of the Imperial Japanese Army were officially over.

On October 25, 1945, the Japanese government retroceded Taiwan and Penghu to the Republic of China (ROC) government, led by the Kuomintang (KMT) party.

Mandarin Chinese was adopted as the national language over Japanese; Taichu was now known as Taichung, and Kiyomizu as Chingshui. All students were at last able to return to school.

Wall: Taichung First Senior High School of Taiwan Province

EVEN IF TIMES HAVE CHANGED, A STUDENT'S ROLE REMAINS THE SAME. YOU MUST CONTINUE TO STUDY AS HARD AS YOU CAN!

Teachers of the "national language" began teaching Pekingese, or Mandarin Chinese, instead of Japanese. Some ethnically Japanese teachers remained at the school, believing it their duty to continue teaching.

THAT'S RIGHT, I MUST WORK HARD! I *FINALLY* GET TO STUDY UNINTERRUPTED!

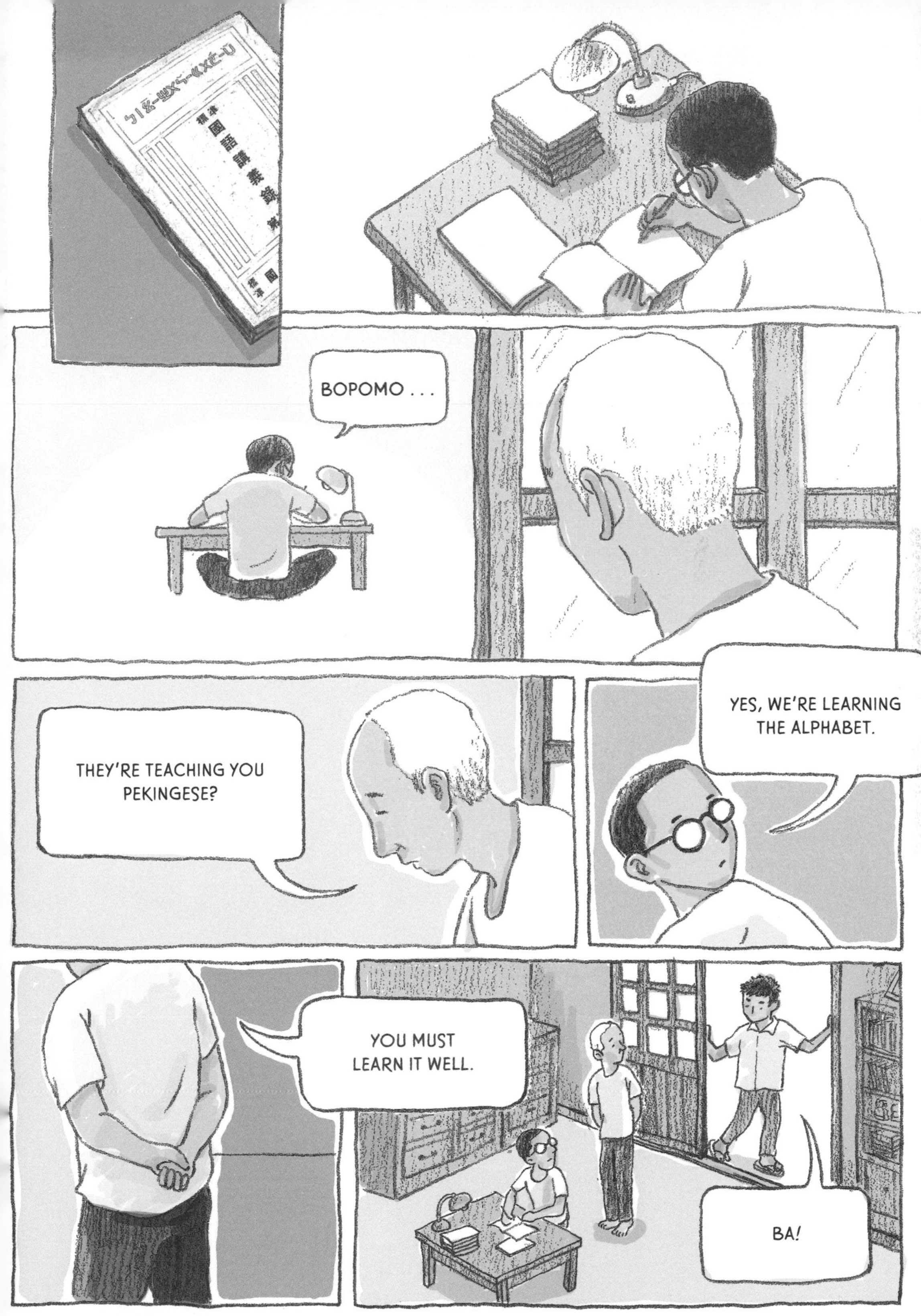
BOPOMO . . .
THEY'RE TEACHING YOU PEKINGESE?
YES, WE'RE LEARNING THE ALPHABET.
YOU MUST LEARN IT WELL.
BA!

THE CHINESE ARMY'S ARRIVED!
?

Top banner: Welcome
Bottom banner: Taiwan Retrocession
歡迎
慶祝光復臺灣

Taiwan thus entered into another era.

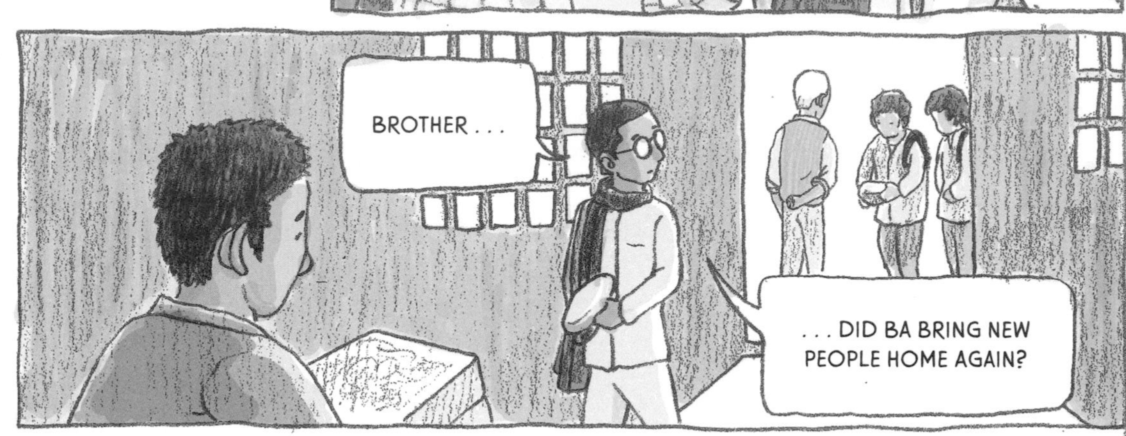

BROTHER . . .
. . . DID BA BRING NEW PEOPLE HOME AGAIN?

YEAH, APPARENTLY THEY CAME FROM FUJIAN ON A LITTLE SAILBOAT. THEY ONLY REACHED GOO-TSHE PORT TWO DAYS AGO.

WHEN BA WAS YOUNG, HE CROSSED THE TAIWAN STRAIT TO XIAMEN AND TRIED TO JOIN AN ORGANIZATION FIGHTING AGAINST THE JAPANESE.

BUT YOUR GRANDMOTHER SENT SOMEONE TO MAKE HIM COME HOME.

歡迎革命青年

第一屆青年夏令營

立國家億萬年不朽之根基

以個人數十年必死之生命

Red banner: Welcome, Revolutionary Youth

August 1946.

Khun-lim graduated from the junior division of his high school and was selected to partake in the First Annual Youth Summer Camp of Taiwan Province held at Tamsui High School.
He, along with roughly five hundred students selected from across Taiwan, trained for one and a half months.

COMMANDER CHEN YI, CHIEF EXECUTIVE AND GARRISON COMMANDER OF TAIWAN PROVINCE, WILL NOW SAY A FEW WORDS.

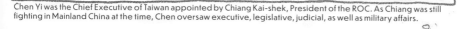

Chen Yi was the Chief Executive of Taiwan appointed by Chiang Kai-shek, President of the ROC. As Chiang was still fighting in Mainland China at the time, Chen oversaw executive, legislative, judicial, as well as military affairs.

第一屆青年夏令營開学典禮

WE HAVE ONE SHARED GOAL:
TO BUILD A NEW CHINA FOUNDED ON
THE THREE PRINCIPLES OF THE PEOPLE.
TAIWAN HAS BEEN IN JAPAN'S ENEMY
HANDS FOR HALF A CENTURY, AND OUR
TAIWANESE COMRADES HAVE GROWN
UNFAMILIAR WITH EVERY ASPECT OF
OUR MOTHERLAND. NOW THAT
RETROCESSION IS COMPLETE, WE WILL
PRIORITIZE THE EDUCATION OF . . .

陳儀

*The Three Principles of the People, developed by Sun Yat-sen, founder of the ROC, are "nationalist union of the people," "government by the people," and "welfare for the people."

CALL OUT YOUR NAMES ONE BY ONE!
?
?
?
DON'T YOU KNOW YOUR OWN NAMES?
YOU THERE, WHAT'S YOUR NAME?
TSAI HUN-LIN.
"HUN"? WHAT CHARACTER?
THE ONE WITH THE FIRE RADICAL.
THAT'S PRONOUNCED "KUN."
AIGH, I EVEN LOOKED IT UP IN THE DICTIONARY!

AS YOUTH, YOU MUST BE CONSCIENTIOUS OF YOUR DUTY TO SAVE THE NATION AND THE WORLD!
YOU MUST BUILD UPON OUR GLORIOUS FIVE-THOUSAND-YEAR HISTORY AND ACTUALIZE THE THREE PRINCIPLES!
YOU ARE OBLIGED TO OUR ANCESTORS AS WELL AS OUR DESCENDANTS!
YOU MUST DEFEND OUR 450 MILLION COMRADES ACROSS THE NATION . . .

?
?
?
?

Interpreter

WHAT HE MEANS IS, WE ALL HAVE TO WORK HARD, AND THE THREE PRINCIPLES ARE REALLY IMPORTANT . . .

Flyer: Three Principles of the People Youth League Member Registration Form

And thus, at fifteen years old, Khun-lim became a party member of the KMT.

Only the top students had been selected to partake in the summer camp.

When the camp concluded in September 1946, Khun-lim was guaranteed admission into the senior division of Taichung First High School.

YOU MUST ALL FOLLOW THE EXAMPLES OF THESE MODEL STUDENTS!
CLAP
CLAP
CLAP
丁一高
CLAP
CLAP
Homeroom teacher Lin Bing-sheng
IT'S DECIDED, THEN. TSAI KUN-LIN WILL BE OUR CLASS LEADER.
OH, BEFORE I FORGET, WE'LL BE HAVING A BONFIRE IN A FEW DAYS.
HURRAH!
ALRIGHT, LET'S START ENGLISH CLASS.
EET KHAN BE EAJILY PROVED JAT NAH-SING IJ MOH PRECIOUS JAN TIME.

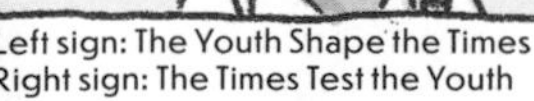
Left sign: The Youth Shape the Times
Right sign: The Times Test the Youth

After the KMT took over, Taiwan experienced economic inflation, food shortages, and political corruption. Even those who had welcomed the new administration soon grew disillusioned.

On February 27, 1947, a government's enforcement team killed one civilian and injured another while investigating contraband cigarettes. The next day, when people gathered in protest, government agents began shooting at the crowd. This escalated into a political conflict now known as the February 28 Incident. Some Taiwanese began resenting the "Waisheng," people who had come from China with the new administration, and the violent persecution of people of Waisheng status became pervasive.

The Horrifying Inspection: Taiwan's February 28 Incident by Huang Rong-can.

Newspaper headline: "Tobacco Enforcement Team Opens Fire on Yanping Road, Killing Civilians"

DID YOU READ THE PAPERS? SOME SOLDIERS SHOT PEOPLE DEAD IN TAIPEI, AND NOW CIVILIAN CONFLICT WITH THE MILITARY IS WORSE THAN EVER.
I HEARD THAT YOU GET ATTACKED JUST FOR BEING WAISHENG.
LISTEN UP, EVERYONE! THINGS ARE TENSE OUT THERE, AND OUR WAISHENG TEACHERS NEED OUR HELP!
HELP ESCORT THE TEACHERS AND THEIR FAMILIES TO THE SCHOOL DORMITORY.
HAVE YOU SEEN MR. LIN?
I HAVEN'T. IS HE OKAY?

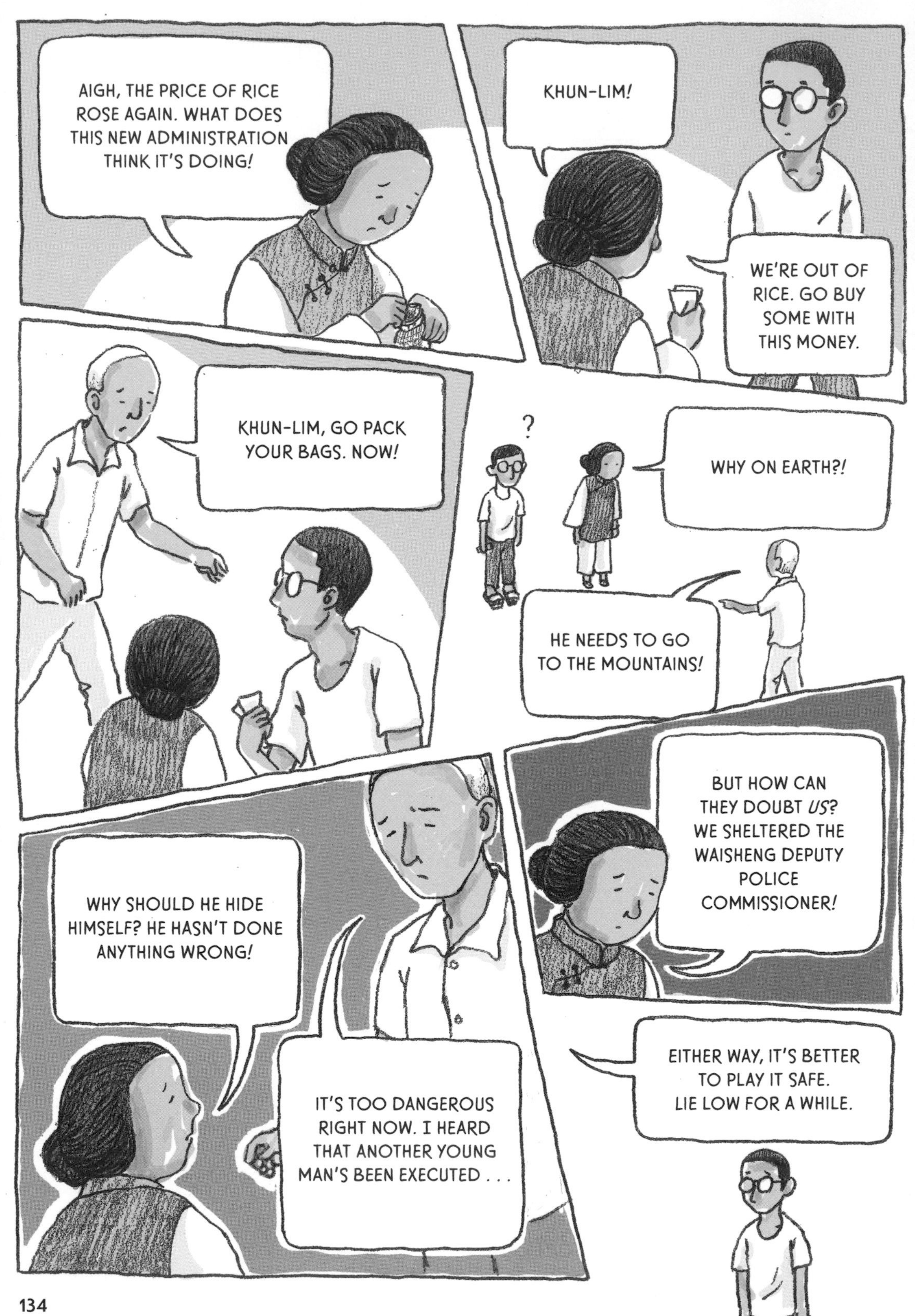
AIGH, THE PRICE OF RICE ROSE AGAIN. WHAT DOES THIS NEW ADMINISTRATION THINK IT'S DOING!
KHUN-LIM!
WE'RE OUT OF RICE. GO BUY SOME WITH THIS MONEY.
KHUN-LIM, GO PACK YOUR BAGS. NOW!
?
WHY ON EARTH?!
HE NEEDS TO GO TO THE MOUNTAINS!
BUT HOW CAN THEY DOUBT *US*? WE SHELTERED THE WAISHENG DEPUTY POLICE COMMISSIONER!
WHY SHOULD HE HIDE HIMSELF? HE HASN'T DONE ANYTHING WRONG!
IT'S TOO DANGEROUS RIGHT NOW. I HEARD THAT ANOTHER YOUNG MAN'S BEEN EXECUTED . . .
EITHER WAY, IT'S BETTER TO PLAY IT SAFE. LIE LOW FOR A WHILE.

The book cover shows "Diary of a Madman," a 1918 short story by Lu Xun, often considered the first work of fiction written in vernacular Chinese. The work attacks traditional Chinese values and calls for a "new culture."

In late April 1947, Chen Yi resigned from his positions as chief executive and garrison commander. President Chiang Kai-shek dissolved the position of chief executive and restructured his government.
On May 15, the newly appointed governor, Wei Tao-ming, arrived in Taiwan. The following day, a new Taiwan Province administration was established. Wei announced an end to the purge and armed suppression. Classes resumed for students.

DID YOU HEAR WE'RE GETTING A NEW HOMEROOM TEACHER? IT'S GOING TO BE THE MATH TEACHER, MR. WANG HAN-CHANG.
實踐三民主義

?
WHAT ABOUT MR. LIN BING-SHENG?

APPARENTLY, HE ESCAPED BACK TO THE MAINLAND WITH HIS GIRLFRIEND.

GIRLFRIEND? THE ENGLISH TEACHER IN THE JUNIOR DIVISION?

YEAH! WORD IS THAT HE'S A COMMUNIST!

!

CLASS IS STARTING!

RISE!

April 1948. Khun-lim's second year of senior high.

One day, in front of the school library . . .

GOOD AFTERNOON, MR. WANG!
TSAI KUN-LIN?
ARE THOSE FROM THE LIBRARY? YOU REALLY DO LOVE TO READ, HUH.
THERE'S A BOOK CLUB IN THE JUNIOR DIVISION, YOU KNOW. ARE YOU INTERESTED?
YESSIR!
THANK YOU, SIR!

NEXT WEDNESDAY, WE'LL EACH PRESENT A BOOK OF OUR CHOICE. ME INCLUDED.

THINK ABOUT WHICH BOOK YOU'D LIKE TO PRESENT.

YOU MEAN THE ONE BY THE BRITISH HISTORIAN THOMAS CARLYLE? YOU CAN READ ENGLISH?
I READ THE JAPANESE TRANSLATION.
THAT'S VERY IMPRESSIVE TOO.
VERY WELL, THAT'S IT FOR TODAY. REMEMBER TO BRING THE BOOKS NEXT WEEK.

MA, WHY ARE YOU STILL UP?

AH, YOU'RE HOME.

HAVE SOME NOODLES.

IT MUST BE TOUGH TAKING THE TRAIN TO SCHOOL EVERY DAY.

CHIRP
PITTER-
PATTER

SPLASH!
SPLASH!
TSAI KUN-LIN! WHAT BOOK DID YOU CHECK OUT TODAY?
MUTUAL AID BY THE RUSSIAN PHILOSOPHER PETER KROPOTKIN.
YOU SURE READ VERY WIDELY! HOW'S THE BOOK CLUB GOING?
SORRY, SIR. I MOVED HOME FROM THE DORMS LAST WEEK AND NEED TO COME BY TRAIN FROM NOW ON, SO I WON'T BE ABLE TO ATTEND ANYMORE.
THAT'S PROBABLY A GOOD THING. FOCUS ON THE UNIVERSITY ENTRANCE EXAM.
SPLASH!
PITTER-PATTER
PITTER-PATTER

With the economy struggling and prices soaring after the war, the Tshua family fell into difficult straits financially. Khun-lim's eldest brother, Khun-ping, went to try his luck in Japan. The third-eldest brother, Khun-tsan, who had moved to Japan for the youth pilot program in Nara, returned to become a teacher at Changhua (formerly "Shoka") Trade School.

WITH KHUN-LIM'S GRADES, HE OUGHT TO GO TO UNIVERSITY.

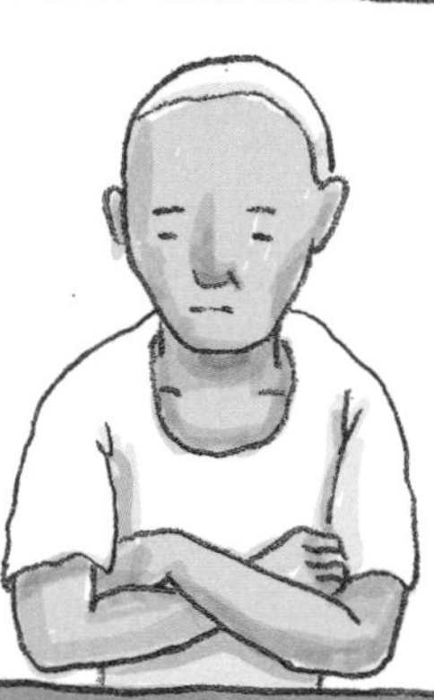

I AGREE. BUT YOU KNOW HOW THINGS ARE FOR OUR FAMILY RIGHT NOW.

KHUN-SIU, WHY DON'T I PAY? KHUN-LIM SHOULD LIVE IN THE DORMS AND FOCUS ON THE ENTRANCE EXAM.

KHUN-TSAN, YOU'VE ONLY JUST STARTED TEACHING. YOUR SALARY ISN'T ENOUGH.

KHUN-LIM, WHAT DO YOU THINK?

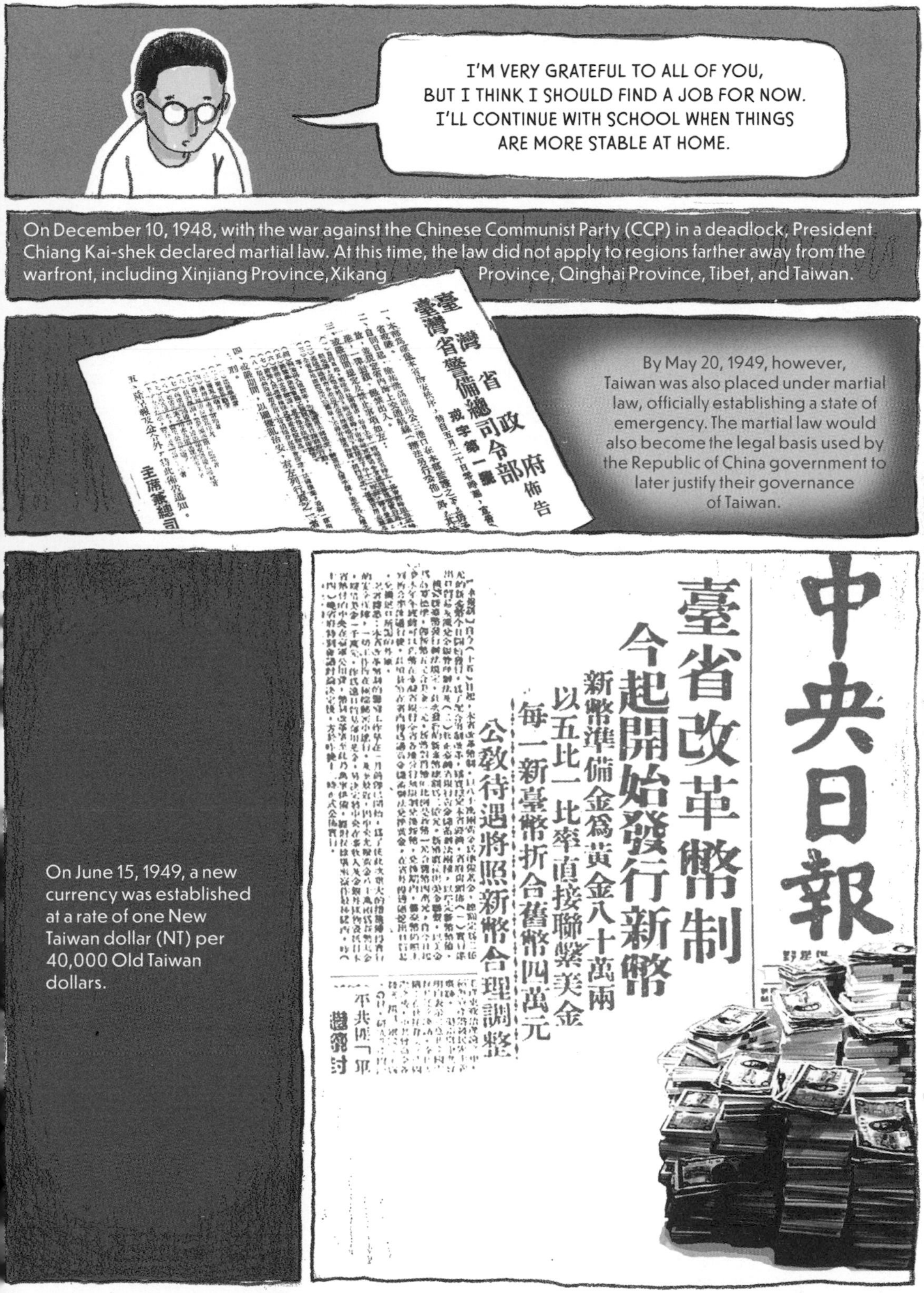

I'M VERY GRATEFUL TO ALL OF YOU, BUT I THINK I SHOULD FIND A JOB FOR NOW. I'LL CONTINUE WITH SCHOOL WHEN THINGS ARE MORE STABLE AT HOME.

On December 10, 1948, with the war against the Chinese Communist Party (CCP) in a deadlock, President Chiang Kai-shek declared martial law. At this time, the law did not apply to regions farther away from the warfront, including Xinjiang Province, Xikang Province, Qinghai Province, Tibet, and Taiwan.

臺灣省政府
臺灣省警備總司令部
佈告
戒字第一號

By May 20, 1949, however, Taiwan was also placed under martial law, officially establishing a state of emergency. The martial law would also become the legal basis used by the Republic of China government to later justify their governance of Taiwan.

On June 15, 1949, a new currency was established at a rate of one New Taiwan dollar (NT) per 40,000 Old Taiwan dollars.

中央日報

臺省改革幣制
今起開始發行新幣
新幣準備金為黃金八十萬兩
以五比一比率直接聯繫美金
每一新臺幣折合舊幣四萬元
公教待遇將照新幣合理調整

In June 1949, Khun-lim graduated from Taichung First High School.
At the Teacher Appreciation Banquet.
TSAI KUN-LIIIN!
ONG CHI-LIN?
YOU'VE ALSO MISSED THE LAST TRAIN HOME, RIGHT? WANNA COME TO THE STADIUM WITH US?
SURE!

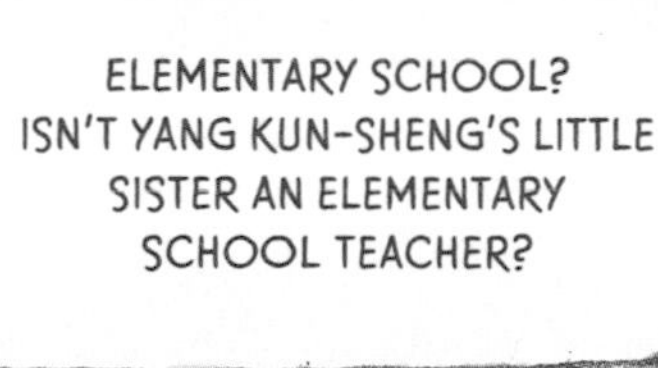

Yang Kun-sheng refers to Khun-lim's old friend Kiyomizu Michio, who had reverted back to his Mandarin Chinese name following the Retrocession. The boys are referring to Khun-lim's crush Kimiko.

I HEARD THAT MR. YANG* WAS ACCUSED OF BEING A TRAITOR? DO YOU KNOW WHAT HAPPENED?

YEAH, HE'S SUSPENDED FROM TEACHING DURING THE INVESTIGATION AND HAS NO INCOME NOW. THAT'S WHY KIMIKO STARTED WORKING RIGHT AFTER JUNIOR HIGH.

Khun-lim did not know why, but everything seemed especially sad to him that night. The starry sky only made him feel even more alone . . .

*Mr. Yang is the Mandarin name of Mr. Kiyomizu, Michio and Kimiko's father and Khun-lim's former teacher.

September 1949. Khun-lim tested into an administrative position at the Chingshui District Office, managing logistics for the military draft.

One month later, the CCP established the People's Republic of China (PRC) in Mainland China. The ROC administration, led by President Chiang Kai-shek, retreated to Taipei in December. A long-lasting standoff began between the two administrations across the Taiwan Strait.

TSAI KUN-LIN,
THE DISTRICT MAYOR IS
ASKING FOR YOU.

KNOCK-
KNOCK

COME IN!

SIR, HOW CAN I BE OF HELP?
KUN-LIN,
LET ME
INTRODUCE
YOU.

THIS IS COMPANY COMMANDER CHEN. HE AND HIS COMPANY HAVE JUST RETREATED FROM HAINAN ISLAND AND ARE LOOKING FOR A PLACE TO STAY.
YOU SPEAK PRETTY GOOD PEKINGESE. YOU HELP HIM LOOK.

JUST SHOW HIM AROUND TOWN.

I'LL TRUST YOU TO HANDLE THIS.
YESSIR.

HOW MANY PEOPLE ARE IN YOUR COMPANY, COMMANDER?
ABOUT A HUNDRED, INCLUDING SOLDIERS AND THEIR FAMILIES.
THAT MANY? THERE ARE ALREADY TROOPS STATIONED AT THE ELEMENTARY SCHOOL . . .
ANY EMPTY BUILDING WILL DO. WE JUST WANT TO REST OUR FEET.

清水鎮公所

THIS WAREHOUSE HAS BEEN EMPTY SINCE THE OWNER MOVED TO THE MAINLAND. YOU CAN STAY HERE FOR NOW.

HOW COULD YOU BE SUCH A FOOL!? I TOLD YOU TO *HANDLE* IT!

IF YOU HADN'T FOUND THEM A PLACE, THEY WOULD'VE GONE TO THE NEXT TOWN! *YOU'RE* GONNA BE THE DEATH OF ME!

DO YOU HAVE *ANY* CLUE HOW MUCH IT'LL COST THE DISTRICT TO FEED A *HUNDRED* PEOPLE?!

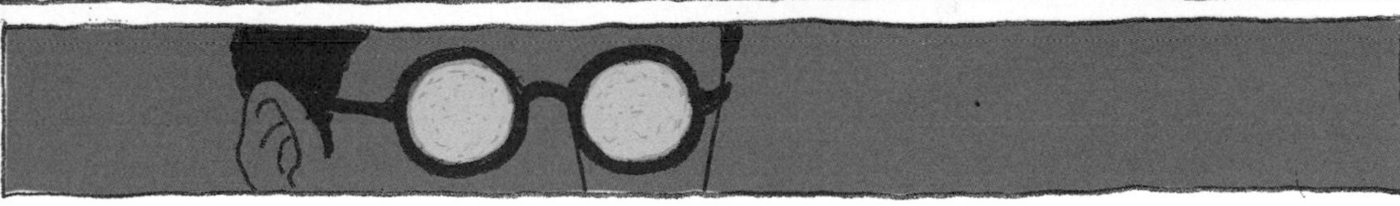

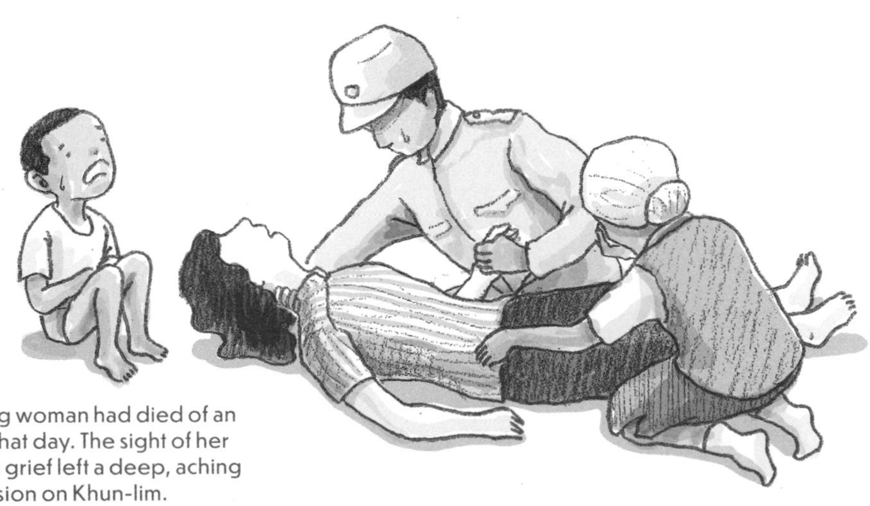

A young woman had died of an illness that day. The sight of her family's grief left a deep, aching impression on Khun-lim.

July 1950.

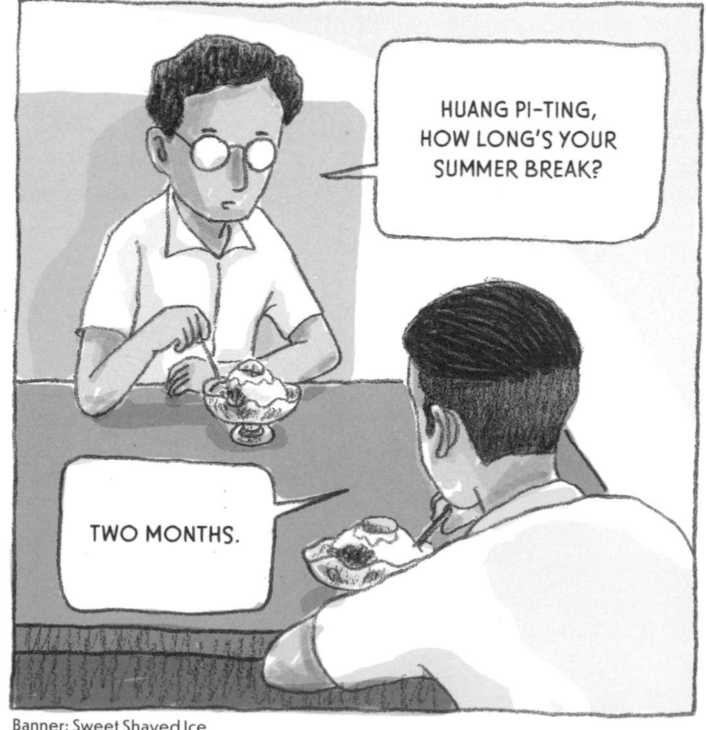

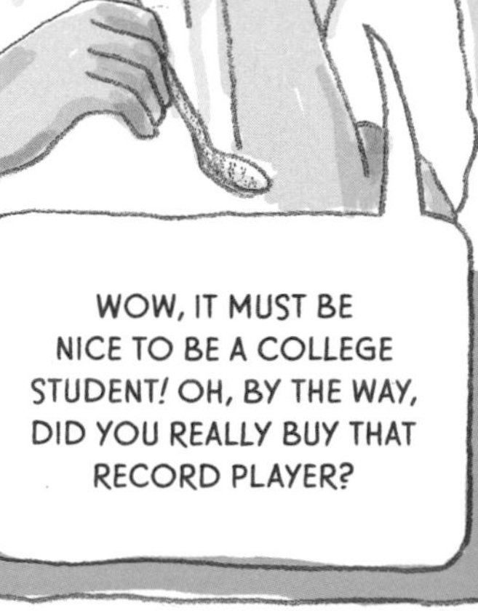

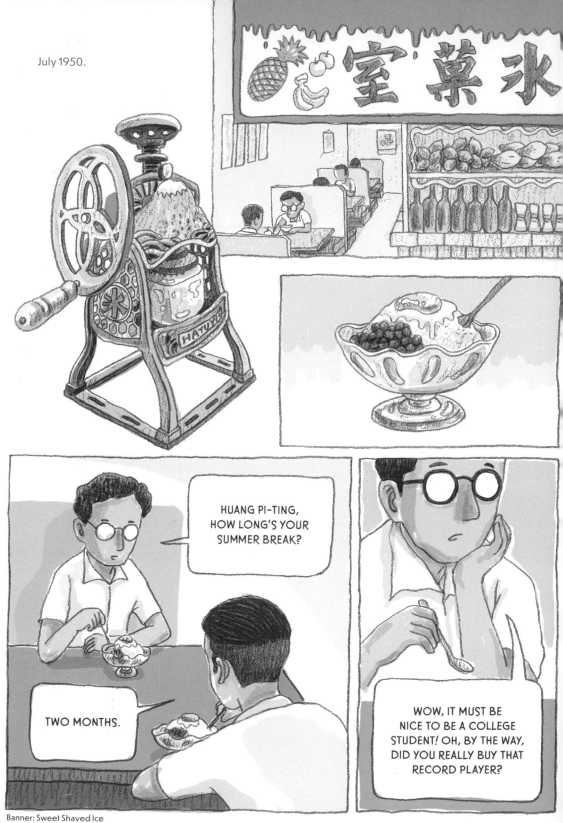

Banner: Sweet Shaved Ice

YEAH, I DID . . .

?

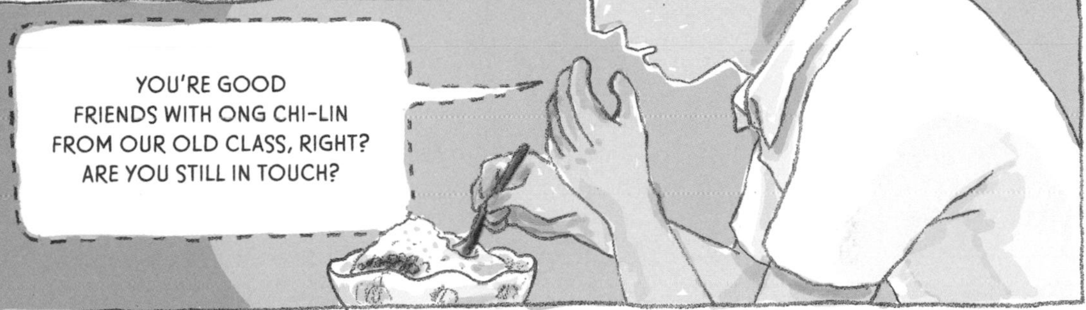
YOU'RE GOOD FRIENDS WITH ONG CHI-LIN FROM OUR OLD CLASS, RIGHT? ARE YOU STILL IN TOUCH?

ISN'T HE WORKING AT A FILM PRODUCTION COMPANY? WHAT'S WRONG?

HE GOT ARRESTED, APPARENTLY. ANY IDEA WHY?

. . . NO IDEA.

September 10, 1950. It was a Sunday with splendid weather. Khun-lim's brother Khun-tsan brought his new wife to the family home in Chingshui.

KHUN-LIM, YOUR HAIR'S GETTING TOO LONG. REMEMBER TO GET IT CUT!

ALRIGHT, ALRIGHT, I'LL GO WHEN I HAVE TIME. I HAVE TO WORK OVERTIME TODAY.

BROTHER, SISTER, PLEASE ENJOY YOURSELVES. I HAVE TO GO TO WORK FOR A BIT, BUT I'LL BE BACK TO HAVE LUNCH WITH YOU.

Left poster: Scatter in Year Three/ Prevail in Year Five
Right poster: Prepare in Year One/ Counterattack in Year Two

KHUN-TSIONG? WHY ARE YOU HERE?
YOUR FRIEND CAME LOOKING FOR YOU AT HOME, SO I BROUGHT HIM HERE.
?
YOU'RE TSAI KUN-LIN?
YES. HOW CAN I HELP YOU?
WHERE'S THE NEAREST POLICE STATION?

Left posters: Keep Secrets, Guard Against Spies
Right posters: Every Citizen Must Do Your Duty

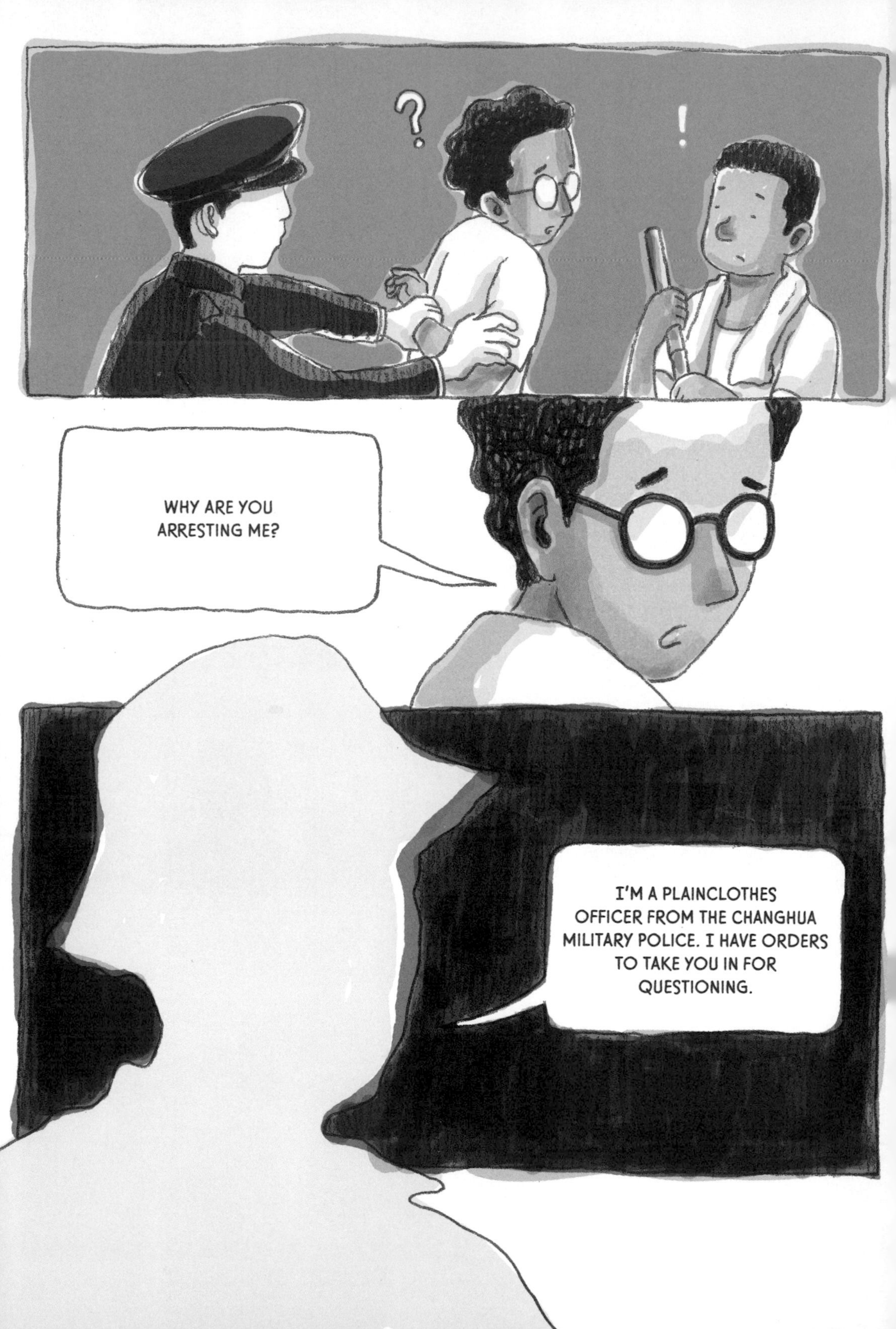
?
!
WHY ARE YOU ARRESTING ME?
I'M A PLAINCLOTHES OFFICER FROM THE CHANGHUA MILITARY POLICE. I HAVE ORDERS TO TAKE YOU IN FOR QUESTIONING.

PART 2
TEN YEARS ON GREEN ISLAND

There is a small island about twenty miles off the southeastern coast of Taiwan.

Formed by the magma of an underwater volcano, the island is roughly six square miles in size. It boasts diverse scenery of mountain ranges, lava formations, cliffs, hot springs, and beaches. Due to the surrounding Black Current in the Pacific Ocean, the island's climate is warm and humid; in the summer, typhoons send waves soaring into the sky, and in the winter, monsoons rage. The air is often dense with sea fog that the locals refer to as "salty rain."

Legend has it that the island's first name was Sanasai, given to it by Austronesian peoples who stopped to rest there on their migration north. In the 19th century, many Han people from Southern China moved to the island and called it Ke-Sim-Su (Chicken Heart Island) and Tshinn-A-Su (Blue-Green Island) in the Hoklo dialect. Later, the Japanese renamed it Kasho-to (Burning Island) and built a vagrants' shelter to hold those deemed harmful to society.

After World War II, the Kuomintang (KMT) administration renamed the island Lyudao (Green Island). They established the New Life Correction Center (1951–1965), and later Green Island Prison (1972–1987)—known as Oasis Villa—to hold political prisoners.

After World War II, the People's Liberation Army, led by the Chinese Communist Party (CCP), launched an attack on the Republic of China (ROC) forces led by the KMT, locking China in a civil war. The KMT held the advantage at first, but the war concluded in their defeat. On October 1, 1949, the CCP established the People's Republic of China (PRC), and by December 8, ROC leaders were forced to retreat to Taiwan, where they became a government-in-exile.

During this time, the rest of the world was entering the Cold War, with communist countries headed by the Soviet Union at odds with capitalist countries headed by the United States. When the Korean War broke out in June 1950, the US sent its Seventh Fleet to defend Taiwan, temporarily alleviating the PRC's threat to the ROC. Chiang Kai-shek, president of the ROC, arrested large numbers of "bandit spies," "rebels," and "Taiwanese independence insurgents" in an effort to strengthen his control over Taiwan. He established a military dictatorship and authoritarian one-party system, thereby launching an era known as the White Terror in Taiwan that would last over forty years.

"They took Khun-lim!" Tshua Khun-lim, who had been working overtime at the District Office, had been arrested by a plainclothes police officer without having committed any crime. His former schoolmate, Tiunn Sing-bo, a custodian at the police station, hurried to the Tshua home to tell them what he had witnessed. Khun-lim's brother, Khun-siu, rushed over to the station, but could get no additional information.

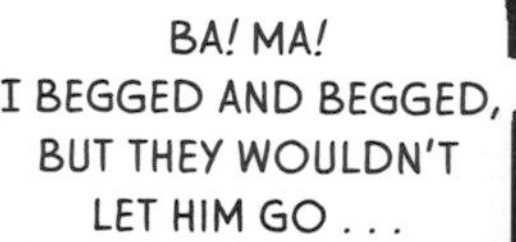

BA! MA! I BEGGED AND BEGGED, BUT THEY WOULDN'T LET HIM GO . . .

AIGH! HOW CAN THIS BE? OFFICER LIN *KNOWS* OUR KHUN-LIM!

I KEPT ASKING THEM WHY, BUT THEY WOULDN'T SAY.
BUT KHUN-LIM IS SO WELL-BEHAVED! HE WORKS FOR THE DISTRICT!

DO YOU KNOW WHERE THEY'RE TAKING HIM?
NO, BUT THEY'RE HEADING TO THE BUS STOP NOW. I'LL GO AND SEE!

KHUN-LIM . . .

BA, MA,
YOU STAY HERE. I'LL
FOLLOW THEM AND SEE
WHERE THEY TAKE HIM!

KHUN-TSAN,
BE CAREFUL!

WHAT CRIME
COULD HE HAVE
COMMITTED?
WHY ARE THEY DRAGGING
MY POOR BOY
LIKE A DOG?

Khun-lim had no idea why he was being seized, nor what awaited him at the end of the bus ride.

He did not know whether he would ever see his family again, or ever confess his love to the girl of his dreams—Kimiko.

KHUN-LIM! KHUN-LIM!

BROTHER . . .

Door sign: Changhua Military Police

Door sign: Interrogation Room

BANG!

F*** YOU!

SLAP!

THUD!

SAY IT!

WHAT CAN I SAY?
I DON'T KNOW ANYTHING . . .

AH!

SIZZLE

JUST FESS UP.
DON'T MAKE ME
HURT YOU.

I REALLY
DON'T KNOW
ANYTHING . . .

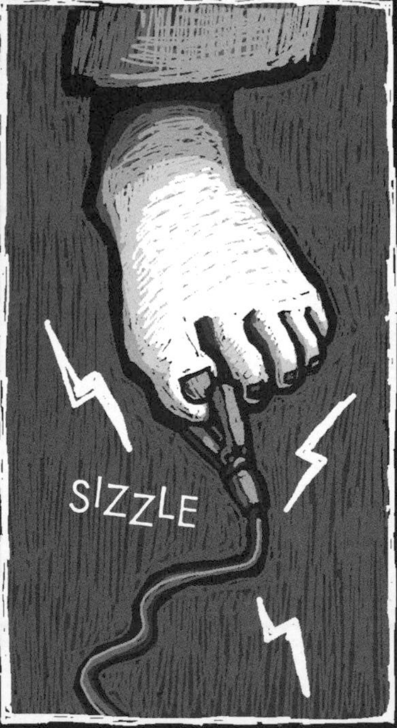
SIZZLE

FAINT

THAT'S AN ILLEGAL ORGANIZATION! IT'S TREASON!

TELL ME,
WHO ELSE WAS IN THIS
ORGANIZATION?

I DIDN'T
KNOW THE OTHERS . . .

GIVE YOURSELF
A BREAK . . .

. . . AND TELL ME
EVERYTHING!

YOU PASSED
OUT FLYERS
FOR THE COMMIES,
DIDN'T YOU?

FLYERS? WHAT?
I DIDN'T!

I NEVER—

WHAM!

WHO WERE THE
OTHER MEMBERS?
WHO WAS THE
ORGANIZER?
HOW DID YOU CONTACT
EACH OTHER?
WHO PASSED OUT
FLYERS WITH YOU?
TELL US EVERYTHING ABOUT
YOUR REBELLIOUS PLANS!

自白書
?
YOU STUDENTS GET GOADED INTO THESE THINGS BECAUSE YOU'RE YOUNG AND IGNORANT.
YOUR FRIENDS HAVE ALL CONFESSED. WHAT'RE YOU HOLDING OUT FOR?
—SIGN THE CONFESSION LETTER—
JUST PRESS YOUR THUMB HERE—
—AND YOU GET TO GO HOME IN TWO DAYS.

After days of torture and interrogation, Khun-lim's body and spirits were on the verge of collapse. He signed his name on the confession letter with its pre-written, made-up crimes and marked it with his thumbprint.

Convicted for espionage, Khun-lim was transferred from the Changhua Military Police to Tainan. Toward the end of September, he was transferred to the Taiwan Provincial Security Command in Taipei.

The Security Command was housed in the former East Hongan Temple, built by the Japanese. It became known as the Asura Purgatory due to the many secret executions carried out there.

The long, narrow individual confinement chambers were like rows of coffins.

It was October, and Taipei's humid and chilly air made Khun-lim shiver from head to toe.

!
TSAI KUN-LIN, YOU'RE UP!
YOU'VE CONFESSED TO JOINING AN ILLEGAL ORGANIZATION AND DISTRIBUTING COMMUNIST FLYERS, CORRECT?
NO, I DIDN'T . . .
YEAH, RIGHT! ISN'T THIS YOUR THUMBPRINT?
THEY SAID THEY'D LET ME GO HOME IF I SIGNED!
SHUT UP!
SIGN HERE!

Not long thereafter, Khun-lim was transferred to the Secrecy Bureau at the Ministry of Defense. The holding cell was only about fifty square feet; with over a dozen prisoners inside, it was overcrowded and overheated.

The Secrecy Bureau was notorious for ruthless torture. In the cell, Khun-lim grew increasingly unnerved by the wails and screams coming from the interrogation room.

In the beginning of October, Khun-lim was transferred to the Detention Center of the Military Law Office for the Taiwan Garrison Command. He would await his sentence there.
There was a field of garden cosmos blossoms at the building's entrance. As Khun-lim walked past, the fuchsia petals swayed to the autumn breeze. He wondered: were the cosmos flowers also in full bloom back home?

Cell number five held twenty-eight men.
The air was unbearably pungent.

LET'S ALL GET SOME EXERCISE!

?

OH, DANNY BOY, THE PIPES, THE PIPES ARE CALLING
FROM GLEN TO GLEN,
AND DOWN THE MOUNTAINSIDE.
THE SUMMER'S GONE, AND ALL THE ROSES FALLING,
'TIS YOU, 'TIS YOU MUST GO AND I MUST BIDE.

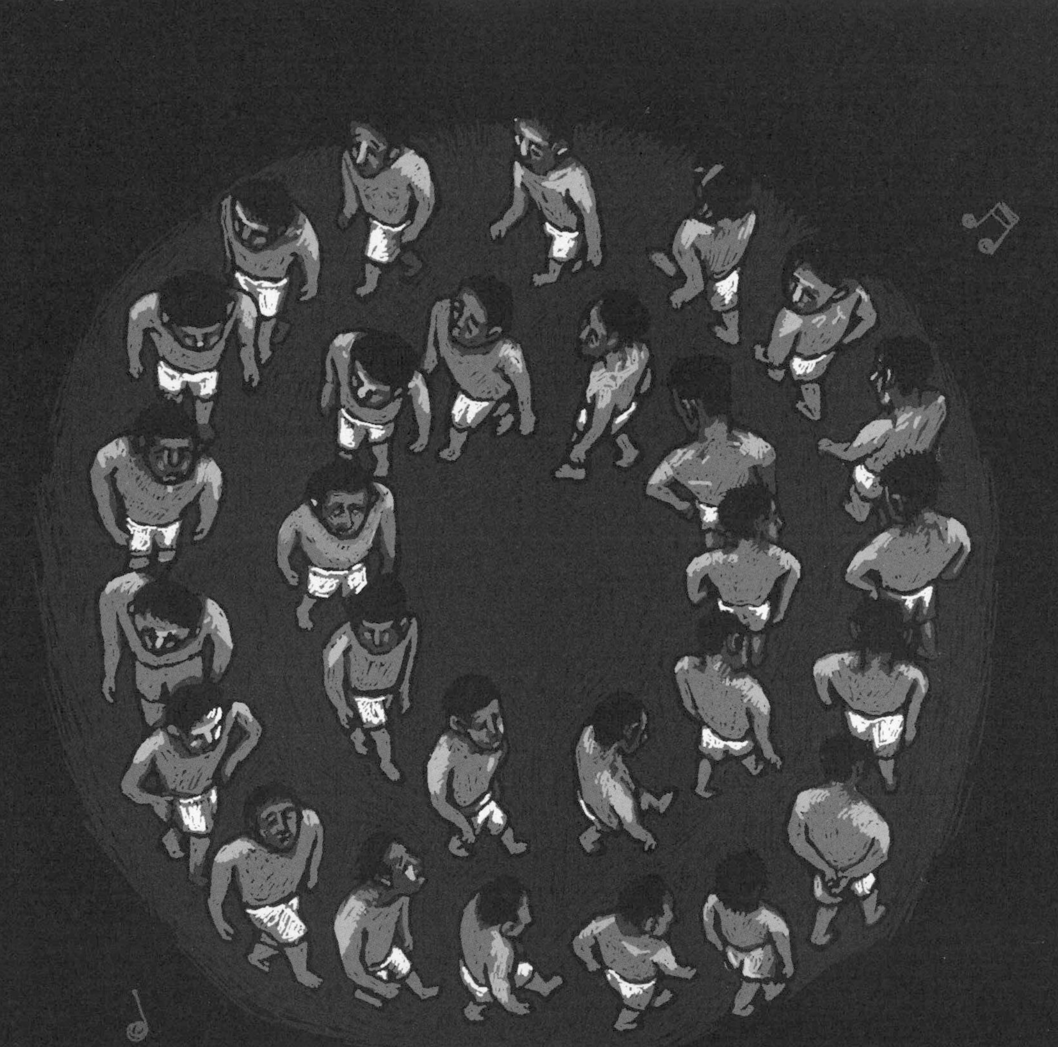

"Danny Boy." Lyrics: Frederic Weatherly. Music: Irish folk song. The lyrics depict a father's feelings as his son heads off to war. In 1913, the songwriter Frederic Weatherly set the poem to the Irish folk song "Londonderry Air," and the ballad became known around the world.

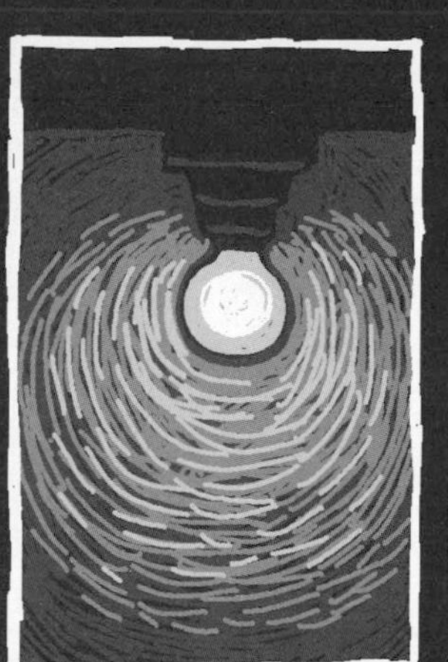

SONNY, THERE'S AN UNOFFICIAL RULE THAT THE LATEST NEWCOMER SLEEPS NEXT TO THE CHAMBER POT. I'M NUMBER TWENTY-SEVEN; YOU'RE TWENTY-EIGHT.
I'M SORRY, BUT YOU'LL HAVE TO BEAR IT TONIGHT.

SONNY! MOVE YOUR HEAD HERE.
GOT A HANDKERCHIEF?

COVER YOUR FACE.

LEE TSANG-CHIANG!

TANG CHI-TANG!

CHONG HAO-TUNG!

IN THE DUSK THE LEAVES FALL
FROM BRANCHES
HITHER AND THITHER ON THE
ROAD LINED WITH TREES
I WATCHED YOUR CARRIAGE GO
LAST YEAR'S PARTING HAS
BECOME ETERNAL
ON THE HILL FULL OF MEMORIES
I GAZE AT THE SKIES OF A
FARAWAY COUNTRY
ONE WHOLE YEAR HAS
DISSOLVED INTO DREAMS
MY TEARS WELL ON AIMLESS DAYS LIKE THESE
THE NOSTALGIC CLATTER OF
PASSING CARRIAGE WHEELS
HITHER AND THITHER ON THE ROAD
LINED WITH TREES
THE WHINNY OF HORSES
ECHOES THROUGH THE WOODS
AND DISAPPEARS INTO A FARAWAY PLACE

Every day, at four or five in the morning, there was a "roll call of death." Prisoners whose names were called were executed next to the Xindian River.

None of the prisoners could predict who would be next.

"The Carriage Song." Lyrics: Yamada Toshiwo. Music: Harano Tameni. Performed by: Wada Haruko. This fast-paced waltz was released in 1932 and was widely played and sung around Japan.

Khun-lim thought about how his uncle's wife had taught him the song when he was a child.

Banners: Justice and Integrity

On November 19, 1950, Khun-lim appeared before the summary court-martial.

The military judge sentenced Khun-lim to ten years imprisonment for the crime of "joining a rebel organization and distributing flyers for rebel traitors."

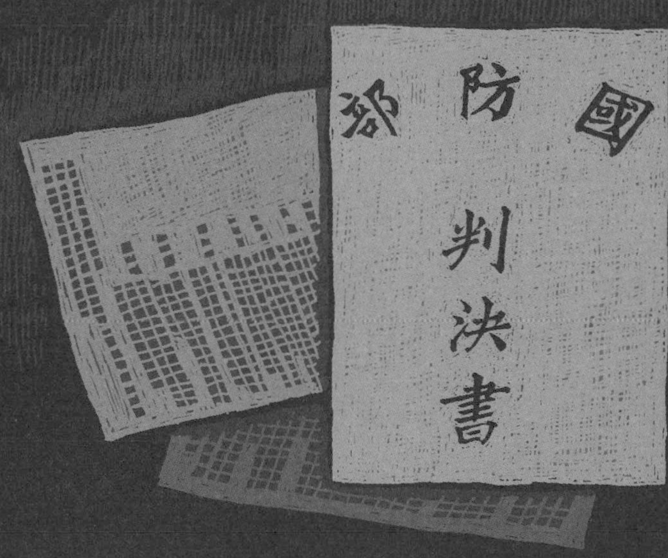

Paper: Ministry of Defense court verdict

KHUN-LIM, WHAT IS IT?

TEN YEARS.
CONGRATULATIONS!
CONGRATULATIONS!

I *TOLD* YOU IT WOULDN'T BE DEATH! CONGRATULATIONS, KHUN-LIM.

MY FAMILY BROUGHT SOME BRAISE-DRIED TOFU TODAY.
COME, EVERYONE SHOULD HAVE SOME.

NOW THAT YOU'VE GOT YOUR VERDICT, YOUR FAMILY CAN COME VISIT YOU TOO.

Despite his fellow prisoners' congratulations, Khun-lim could not bring himself to feel glad about being separated from his loved ones for ten years due to crimes he never committed.

KHUN-LIM, CAN YOU DO ME A FAVOR?

?

IF MY NAME IS CALLED, PLEASE SEND THIS BLANKET TO MY FAMILY . . . AS SOMETHING TO REMEMBER ME BY.

The Military Justice Department allowed family visits after a prisoner received their verdict. Khun-lim's second-eldest brother, Khun-siu, applied to see him.

Khun-lim was finally reunited with family after what felt like a lifetime.

TELL THEM THAT THEY DON'T HAVE TO WORRY ABOUT ME EITHER.

BROTHER.
CAN YOU PLEASE . . . SEND THIS BLANKET TO THIS ADDRESS HERE . . .

REST IN PEACE, DEPARTED COMRADE! WORRY FOR OUR MOTHERLAND NO MORE.

YOUR BLOOD HAS LIT THE PATH THAT WILL GUIDE US FORWARD.

YOU ARE THE PRIDE OF DEMOCRACY.

YOU HAVE SACRIFICED MUCH OUT OF LOVE TO YOUR COUNTRY.

THE BLEAK WINDS OF WINTER WILL ROCK THE CRADLE OF SPRING.

"The Song of Peaceful Rest." Originally titled "Rest in Peace, My Departed Classmate." The song was composed to memorialize Chinese university students who were killed in 1945 while protesting the civil war, an event known as the Kunming December 1 Incident. During the White Terror era in Taiwan, it was adapted into a farewell song for those killed.

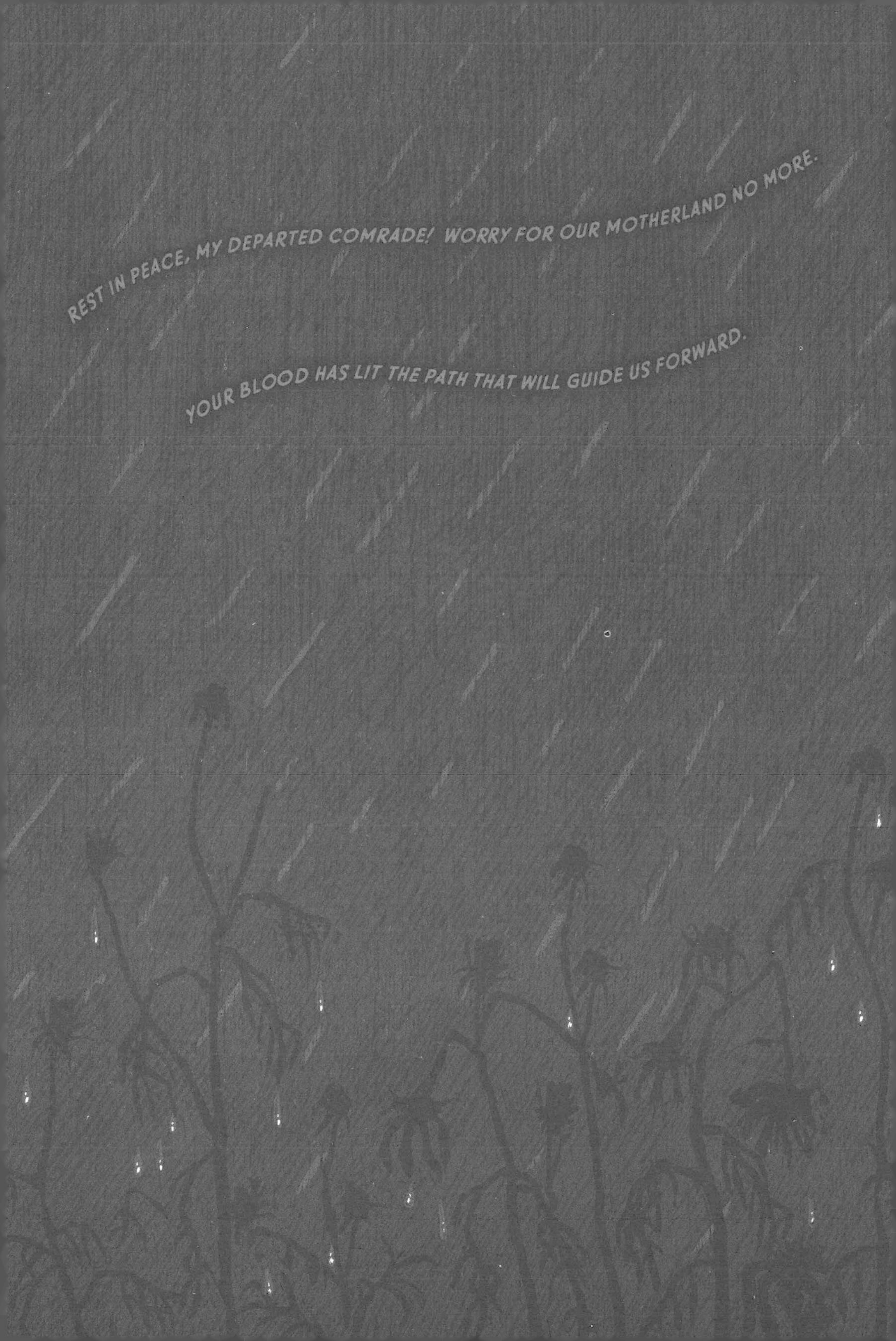

REST IN PEACE, MY DEPARTED COMRADE! WORRY FOR OUR MOTHERLAND NO MORE.

YOUR BLOOD HAS LIT THE PATH THAT WILL GUIDE US FORWARD.

After the Industrial Revolution, socialist sentiments grew increasingly prevalent in response to corruption and other shortcomings of capitalist systems. In the 19th century, socialist movements flourished around the world, advocating for peace, social transformation, and the welfare of the working masses. At the time, socialism still allowed for private property. Later, communism, founded on Karl Marx's ideas, would promote even more radical means to eradicate social inequality such as public property, class struggle, and the use of force. Whether moderate or radical, left-wing movements dominated intellectual thought in the 20th century.

Under the Japanese, many of Taiwan's intellectuals were likewise influenced by leftist thought and launched social reform movements that pushed back against colonial rule. Socialist and communist ideas remained popular in Taiwan after World War II, and many utopian works were widely circulated, including those of Ishikawa Takuboku, Arishima Takeo, Leo Tolstoy, Victor Hugo, Lu Xun, and Mao Dun. Many of these books were especially beloved by high school students like Khun-lim.

However, after the KMT moved to Taiwan in 1949, it began arresting large numbers of Chinese Communist "bandit spies" and openly prioritized the purging of left-wing ideology as the first step toward stabilizing their control over Taiwan. As a result, all of the above books were banned. Anyone who criticized the KMT or read books deemed leftist, socialist, or communist could be persecuted for violation of the Statutes for the Punishment of Rebellion and the Statutes for the Detection and Eradication of Spies During the Period of Communist Rebellion Act.

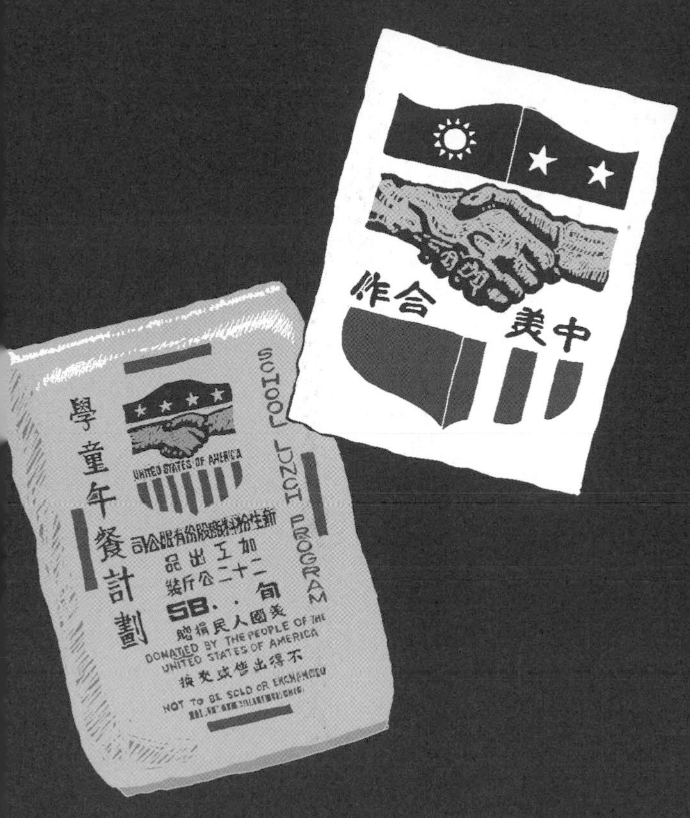

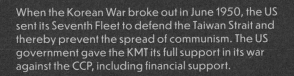

When the Korean War broke out in June 1950, the US sent its Seventh Fleet to defend the Taiwan Strait and thereby prevent the spread of communism. The US government gave the KMT its full support in its war against the CCP, including financial support.

In the meantime, due to President Chiang Kai-shek's heavy-handed policies in response to the February 28 Incident, many Taiwanese became disillusioned with the KMT and began to support communist ideas. Some even joined underground CCP organizations. The KMT military, police, and secret police adopted a policy of "better to kill a hundred innocents than to let one criminal escape," and carried out sweeping and intensive searches, frame-ups, arrests, interrogations, torture, forced confessions, and unjust military trials. Almost every week, people were shot on Taipei's Machangding Execution Grounds for false or erroneous charges.

MA . . .

MA . . .

MA, PLEASE TAKE THIS TO THE GODDESS AND ASK HER PROTECT BROTHER KHUN-LIM.

請觀音菩薩保佑
哥哥蔡焜霖
早日回來

KHUN-TSIONG, YOU SILLY, SILLY BOY! LEADING THAT POLICE OFFICER TO YOUR BROTHER . . .

After Khun-lim's arrest, his mother had begun visiting the bodhisattva Guanyin's temple at five o'clock every morning to pray.
She could not forgive Khun-lim's younger brother Khun-tsiong, and Khun-tsiong, who likewise blamed himself, had cut his finger and used his own blood to write a letter to the goddess praying for Khun-lim's safe return.

As the number of arrests continued escalating, the jails and prisons ran out of space. Public places like theaters were converted into makeshift detention centers.

In early January 1951, Khun-lim was transferred to one such facility at the Xindian Theater.

On March 10, at around noon, Khun-lim's father, Tshua Mi-hong, applied to visit him.

Father and son gazed at each other through a small window. Neither spoke for a long time.

BA . . . DID YOU COME ALONE?

YOUR SISTER'S HUSBAND CAME WITH ME.

IS MA DOING WELL?

MM.

I BROUGHT SOME THINGS SHE MADE FOR YOU.

BA . . .

DON'T WORRY!

IT MIGHT BE TEN YEARS, BUT . . .
. . . AT LEAST IT'S NOT DEATH, AND . . .
. . . IF I BEHAVE WELL, THEY'LL LET ME OUT EARLY . . .
KHUN-LIM, MY BOY, YOU MUST TAKE GOOD CARE OF YOURSELF . . . OF YOUR HEALTH . . .

Not long after the meeting with his father, Khun-lim was returned to the Military Law Office Detention Center.

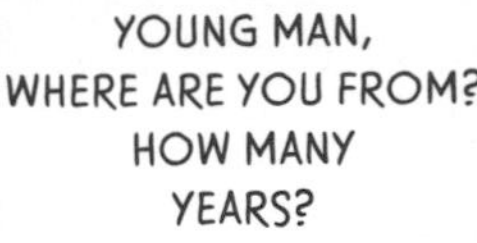

YOUNG MAN, WHERE ARE YOU FROM? HOW MANY YEARS?

I'M FROM TAINAN, ALSO TEN YEARS. YOU'RE STILL YOUNG, BUT I'LL BE FORTY BY THE TIME I'M OUT.

IUNN GIN-SIONG, WILL YOU TELL US YOUR *POW* STORIES WITH THE AUSTRALIANS AGAIN?
POW?

YEAH, I SERVED IN THE JAPANESE ARMY IN THE SOUTH PACIFIC.

WE FOUGHT IN THE TROPICAL JUNGLE IN PAPUA NEW GUINEA.

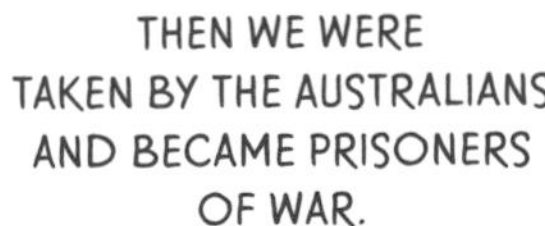

THEN WE WERE TAKEN BY THE AUSTRALIANS AND BECAME PRISONERS OF WAR.

BUT THE AUSTRALIANS WEREN'T SO BAD. WE NEVER WENT HUNGRY, AND THEY TAUGHT US HOW TO TAP DANCE.

TAP DANCE?
YEAH. I'LL SHOW YOU.

Khun-lim marveled at how Iunn Gin-siong could maintain such a positive attitude after everything he'd been through.
I never expected to meet so many people I can look up to in prison.

Two days later, Khun-lim was transferred to
the newly established New Life Correction
Headquarters at the Neihu Elementary School.

Those considered political criminals were sent to concentration camps for thought reform and reeducation. Beginning in 1950, a public school campus in Neihu was reconfigured into the Neihu New Life Corps by the Garrison Command for this purpose.

Board: The Three Principles of the People
Nationalist union of the people
Government by the people
Welfare for the people

COUNTERATTACK, COUNTERATTACK: RETAKE THE MAINLAND!
COUNTERATTACK, COUNTERATTACK: RETAKE THE MAINLAND!
THE MAINLAND IS OUR COUNTRY, THE MAINLAND IS OUR TERRITORY
OUR COUNTRY, OUR TERRITORY
WE WILL RETAKE IT! WE WILL RETAKE IT!
COUNTERATTACK, COUNTERATTACK! RECLAIM THE MAINLAND, RECLAIM THE MAINLAND!

"Retake the Mainland." Lyrics: Jing Shu. Music: Li Zhong-he. A political-education song promoted by the ROC government for inspiring counteroffensive sentiments.

Compared to the crowded and windowless cells of the detention centers, the concentration camp at Neihu brought Khun-lim slightly more comfort. At the very least, the sight of the blue sky relieved some of the frustrations pent up in his body and soul.

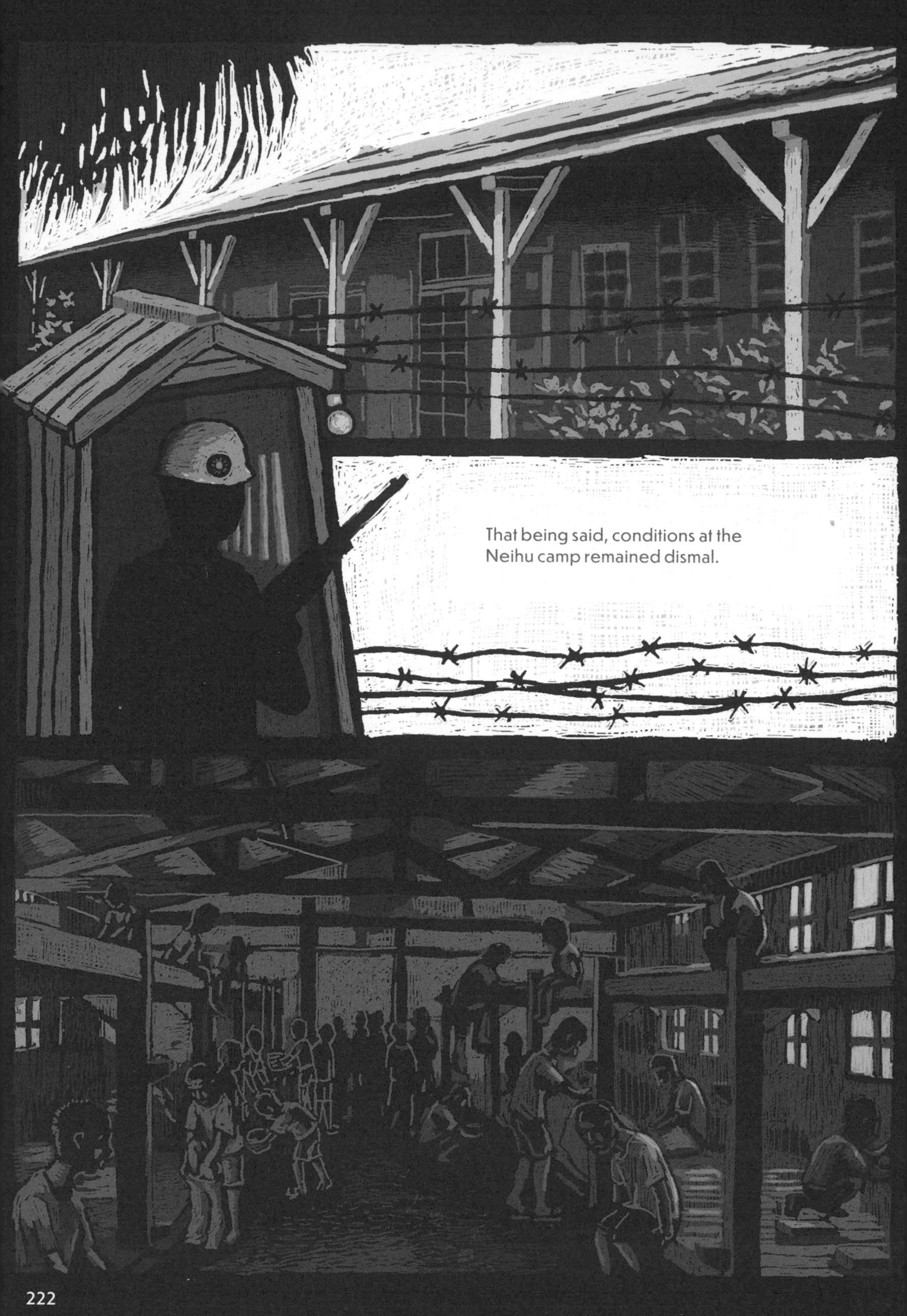
That being said, conditions at the
Neihu camp remained dismal.

May 15, 1951. At the crack of dawn, roughly one thousand political prisoners—Khun-lim among them—were taken from the reeducation camp at Neihu and the detention center at Xindian to an amphibious landing ship at Keelung Harbor. Each convict was only allowed one knapsack of bare necessities and two steamed buns.

The ship set sail. Its passengers knew nothing of their destination.

This was a tank landing ship that the US Army gave to the ROC after World War II. The ship's bottom was flat, making it rock more. The windowless bilge, where the prisoners were held during the journey, was originally used to store military tanks and other supplies.

WHERE ARE WE GOING?

ARE WE GOING TO ANOTHER COUNTRY?

WHERE ARE THEY TAKING US?

WHAT IF THEY DUMP US IN THE MIDDLE OF THE OCEAN?

AS LANDFILL?

BLEGH!

...

...

...

WAIT . . .
THE BUN'S ALL MOLDY . . .

GET IN LINE!
COME UP ONE
BY ONE!

After an unknown number of days in the unlit bilge,
Khun-lim's eyes were dazzled by sunlight.
He saw that he was surrounded by clear,
blue water with a small, verdant island before him.

Have we gone from hell to heaven? he wondered.

Khun-lim recognized the name.
He'd heard that Hsieh Kui-fang's older brother, Hsieh Kui-lin, was a doctor who'd already been executed.

Two months after their arrival on the island, Hsieh Kui-fang, with his radiant smile that brought such consolation to Khun-lim, died of liver disease.

White cockroaches: sea cockroaches, isopods common on the coastline.

Due to the tropical climate of Green Island, its residents did not dress in Han Chinese clothes. They'd been told to expect a group of lawless Xinsheng (meaning "New Lifers"), the pronunciation of which is similar to "gorilla" in Taiwanese Hoklo. They had been warned not to approach these dangerous criminals.

Entrance sign: Home for New Lifers

Green Island, an island in the Pacific that is only sixteen square kilometers, was inhabited by Hoklo people who had migrated there from Liuqiu Island. It was formerly known as Burning Island under the Japanese.
In 1951, the Taiwan Provincial Security Command established the New Life Correction Center and relocated most political prisoners here.

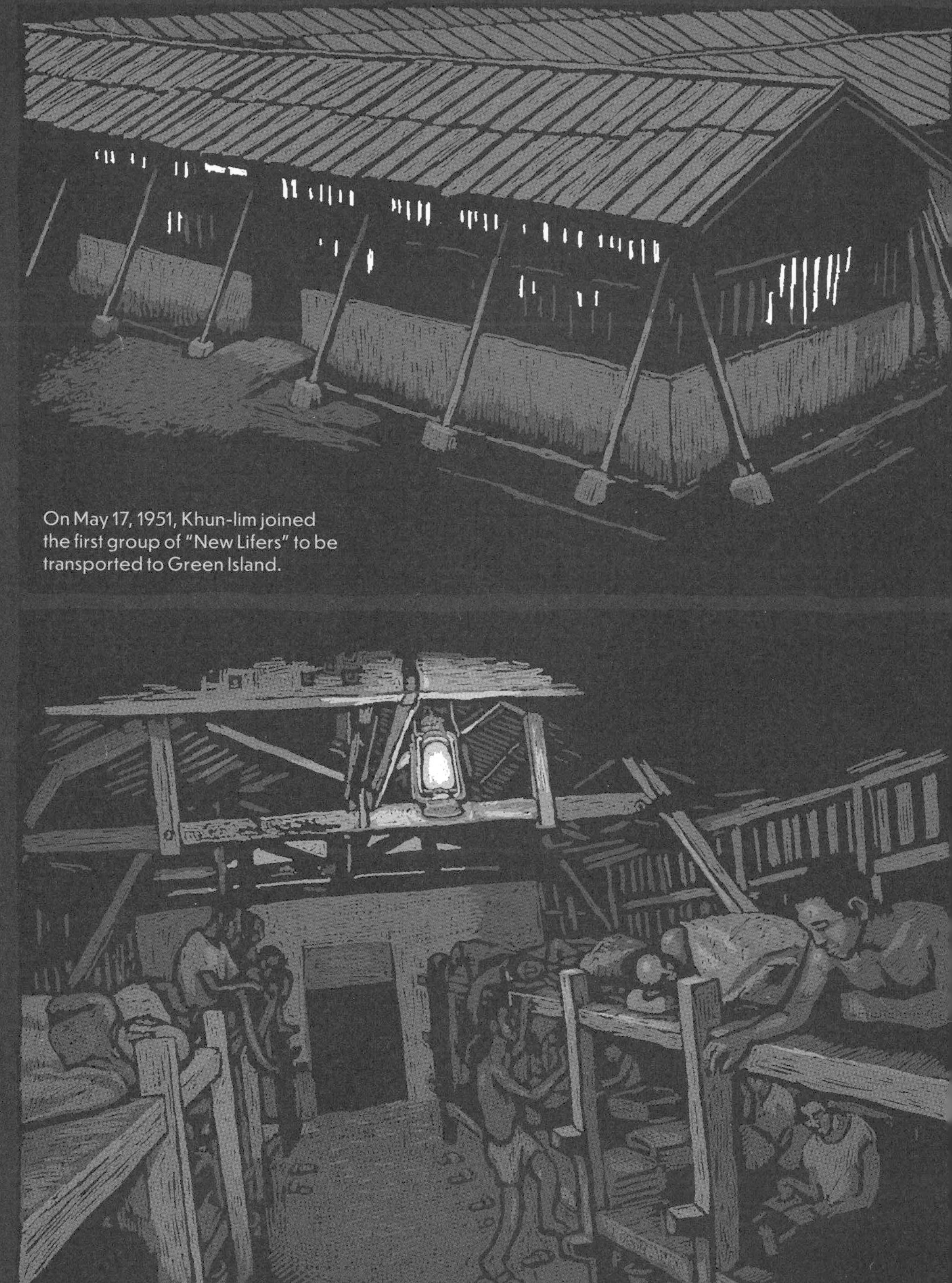

On May 17, 1951, Khun-lim joined the first group of "New Lifers" to be transported to Green Island.

That night, for the first time since his arrest eight months prior, Khun-lim was able to sleep with his legs fully stretched out. Even so, thinking of his home, his parents, and Kimiko, he felt the tears build behind his eyes.

The following morning.

COMRADES, I AM THE DIRECTOR OF THE NEW LIFE CORRECTION CENTER. OUR BENEVOLENT GOVERNMENT HAS GRANTED YOU A CHANCE TO REFORM YOUR MINDS HERE AND WASH YOUR HANDS CLEAN OF YOUR CRIMES.

Major General Yao Sheng-chai, the first director of the New Life Correction Center.

MARK MY WORDS! I REPRESENT A CROSSROADS. THOSE WHO FOLLOW ME WILL LIVE; THOSE WHO TURN THEIR BACKS TO ME WILL DIE!

There were roughly two thousand people in the correction center. They were divided into three brigades, with four squadrons in each brigade. There was a smaller and separate women's squad.

Khun-lim was put into Brigade 1, Squadron 3.

Due to construction needs and the lack of resources, New Lifers were made to perform hard labor by the seaside from morning to night.

BANG!

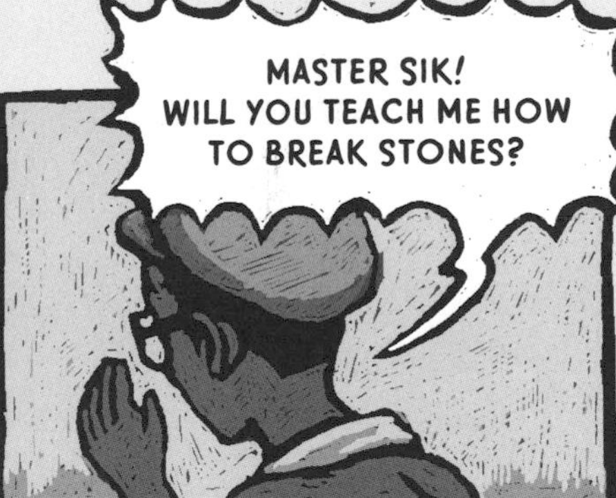

MASTER SIK!
WILL YOU TEACH ME HOW TO BREAK STONES?

!

YOU'RE TOO SKINNY; YOU WON'T HAVE THE STRENGTH.
COME ON, LET ME TRY.

ALRIGHT, IF YOU WANT.
TAKE GOOD AIM!
BANG!

GOOD! AGAIN!

?

ON SECOND THOUGHT, I'LL JUST DO THE LIFTING.

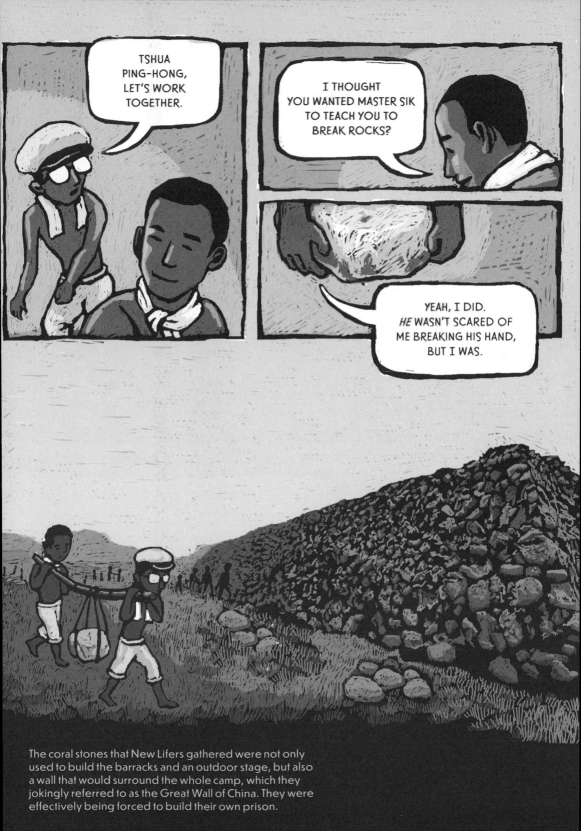

The coral stones that New Lifers gathered were not only used to build the barracks and an outdoor stage, but also a wall that would surround the whole camp, which they jokingly referred to as the Great Wall of China. They were effectively being forced to build their own prison.

TODAY'S TOPIC IS THE 37.5 RENT REDUCTION PLAN. TSAI KUN-LIN WILL ACT AS NOTETAKER. EVERYBODY HAS TO SPEAK.

THE GOVERNMENT, UH, DIC-DICTATES THAT TENANT FARMERS ONLY NEED TO PAY A MAX . . . MAXIMUM OF 37.5 PERCENT OF THEIR ANNUAL HARVEST TO THEIR LANDLORDS. THE NEW . . . P-POLICY ALSO PROTECTS TENANT FARMERS FROM . . . UH . . .

UPHOLDS THE RIGHT-TO-FARM LAWS.
UP-UPHOLDS THE RIGHT-TO-FARM LAWS OF . . .

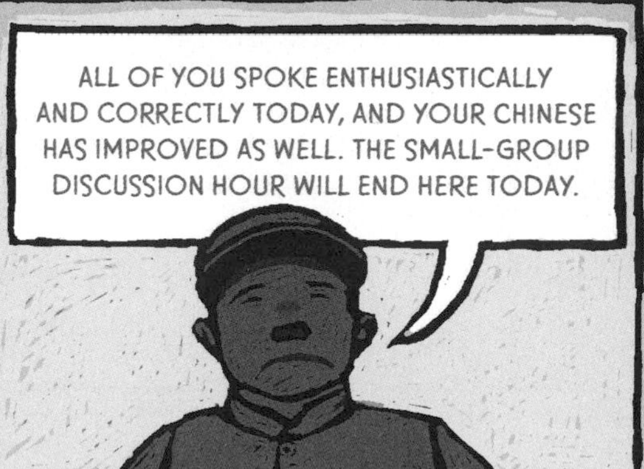

ALL OF YOU SPOKE ENTHUSIASTICALLY AND CORRECTLY TODAY, AND YOUR CHINESE HAS IMPROVED AS WELL. THE SMALL-GROUP DISCUSSION HOUR WILL END HERE TODAY.

THANK GOODNESS YOU HELPED ME WRITE THE SCRIPT LAST NIGHT! AND PRACTICED CHINESE WITH ME!

In addition to the grueling small-group discussions, New Lifers also had to attend political reform lessons on the teachings of the late Sun Yat-sen, founder of the Republic of China. The lessons also spanned historical Soviet invasions of China, Communist atrocities, new land policies, the 375 Rent Reduction Plan, and critiques of Mao Zedong.

OUR LEADER CHIANG KAI-SHEK RESOLVED TO SAVE HIS COUNTRY AND COUNTRYMEN AT AN EARLY AGE. HE THREW HIMSELF INTO REVOLUTIONARY WORK AT AGE EIGHTEEN, AND . . .

THE POLITICAL THEORIST YEH CH'ING WROTE THAT SO-CALLED "MAOISM" IS "CHINA'S PROLETARIANISM," AND MAO IS THE MODERN EQUIVALENT OF THE CULTIST AND REBEL TYRANT HONG XIUQUAN!
THAT'S WHAT *PROLETARIAT* MEANS? TAKING THE SIDE OF THE PEASANTS?

IN HIS FALLACIOUS SPEECH "ON THE PEOPLE'S DEMOCRATIC DICTATORSHIP," THE CRIMINAL MAO CLAIMED: "THE PEOPLE NEED THE LEADERSHIP OF THE WORKING CLASS, FOR THE WORKING CLASS ALONE IS MOST FARSIGHTED, SELFLESS, AND THOROUGHLY REVOLUTIONARY . . . NO OTHER CLASS CAN SUCCESSFULLY LEAD A TRUE REVOLUTION."
匪黨理論批判、杜撰、新民主主義
THIS IS ENTIRELY MISTAKEN! A TOTAL FALLACY!

PROLETARIAT? WORKERS' AND PEASANTS' REVOLUTION? MARXISM?

Though imprisoned for being a Communist spy, Khun-lim did not know anything about Mao Zedong's "criminal" ideas until learning about them in political reform classes.

MR. WANG?

MR. WANG HAN-CHANG!

!

SIR, IT'S ME, TSAI KUN-LIN!

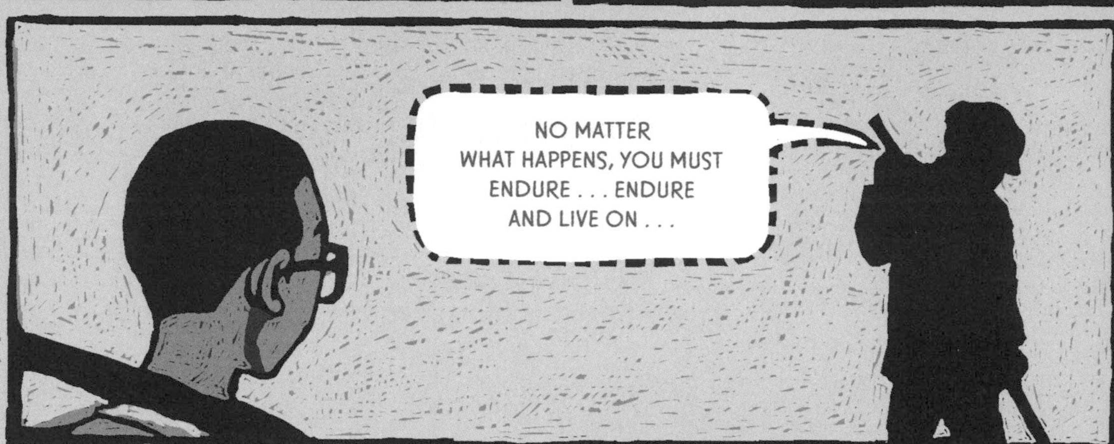

Prisoners in different brigades were forbidden from speaking to one another.

Khun-lim happened upon Mr. Wang Han-chang, his high school teacher who'd introduced him to the book club, while on an errand.

It would be his last time ever seeing Mr. Wang.

*Liuma Channel: The water source for roughly two thousand people living in the correction center.

PROFESSOR AU-IONG BUN IS A PAINTER, AND HE'S GOOD AT PHOTOGRAPHY TOO.

IT'S A SECRET, BUT I'VE HIDDEN A BOTTLE OF WHISKEY UNDER MY BED BACK HOME.

WHEN I GET OUT, I'LL WAIT FOR PROFESSOR AU-IONG TO OPEN IT AND CELEBRATE.

IT'S 9:30! TO THE SLEEPING QUARTERS!
HEY, KHUN-LIM, DO ME A FAVOR. MY FAMILY SENT THIS LETTER, BUT I CAN'T READ. WOULD YOU READ IT OUT LOUD FOR ME?
SURE.
THANK YOU.
IT'S NOTHING!

蔡焜霖收
KHUN-LIM,
ARE YOU ALRIGHT?
TAN ING-THAI.
I'M FINE.
MY FAMILY WROTE TO SAY
THAT EVERYTHING'S FINE
BACK HOME.
ONLY . . .
BECAUSE OF ME,
MY YOUNGEST BROTHER
CAN'T GO TO HIGH SCHOOL.
HE'S NOW SELLING SOY SAUCE
ON A BICYCLE TO HELP WITH
THE FAMILY INCOME . . .

KHUN-LIM, CAN YOU HELP ME WRITE A LETTER?

BUT, KHUN-LIM, YOU'RE QUITE THE WILD SLEEPER! YOUR FOOT ENDED UP ON MY STOMACH HALFWAY THROUGH THE NIGHT!

HAHAHA . . . SORRY ABOUT THAT!

The mutual care and affection among fellow New Lifers gave Khun-lim the courage and patience to withstand his imprisonment.

COMRADES,
OUR GREAT LEADER,
PRESIDENT CHIANG KAI-SHEK,
HAS RECENTLY ANNOUNCED
THE FOLLOWING:

YOU HAVE SHOWN DEDICATION
THESE PAST FEW MONTHS IN STUDYING
THE CORRECT IDEAS. THE GOVERNMENT IS
BENEVOLENT, AND YOU HAVE ALL BEEN GRANTED
THE CHANCE FOR A NEW LIFE. SO LONG AS YOU
CONTINUE WITH THE GOOD WORK,
YOUR TRAINING HERE MAY COME TO AN END
WHEN A NEW ORDINANCE PASSES.

EVERY PERSON IS TO COLLECT ONE LARGE BUNDLE AND MEET BACK HERE IN TWO HOURS. DISMISSED!

THE MOUNTAIN WHERE I ONCE CHASED RABBITS, THE RIVER WHERE I ONCE CAUGHT GOLDFISH
I CAN ONLY SEE THEM IN MY DREAMS NOW MY UNFORGETTABLE HOMETOWN
HOW ARE YOU, DEAR PARENTS? ARE YOU WELL, OLD PLAYMATES?
I THINK OF MY HOMETOWN WHENEVER THE WIND BLOWS AND THE RAIN FALLS
IF I CAN ACHIEVE MY DREAMS THEN ONE DAY I SHALL RETURN
TO THE BLUE-GREEN HILLS OF MY HOMETOWN TO THE CLEAR WATERS OF MY HOMETOWN

"Hometown." Lyrics: Takano Tatsuyuki. Music: Okano Teiichi. A Japanese children's song released in 1914 that was included in a music textbook for Japanese sixth-grade students.

!

CAREFUL!

MASTER SIK!
I OWE YOU MY LIFE!
DON'T EXAGGERATE!

THATCH FOR
THE BARRACKS GOES THERE!
SHELL-FLOWER LEAVES FOR
ROPES GO HERE!
TAKE A
TEN-MINUTE BREAK
AFTER!

TSAI KUN-LIN!
?

OVER HERE!
COME.

During the Korean War, from 1950 to 1953, there were rumors among Waisheng prisoners that the KMT in Mainland China had started a practice of setting fire to concentration camps whenever they had a major retreat. They feared that, should the KMT feel compromised by the Korean War, all political prisoners would be executed.

Each squadron elected three members to the canteen committee every month. Khun-lim, who knew accounting, was put in charge of shopping for ingredients, including going to the port to buy fish.

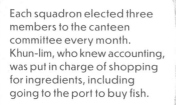

Nanliao Fishing Harbor.

"KOREAN WAR ESCALATES; COMMUNIST BANDITS CONDUCT EXPLORATORY SEARCHES; ALLIES KILL OVER TWO HUNDRED . . ."

"A 'MATRILINEAL SOCIETY' IS FOUNDED ON THE PRIMITIVE COMMUNAL SYSTEM. IN A COMMUNIST FAMILY, EVERY PERSON IS EQUAL."
"A 'PATRILINEAL SOCIETY' IS FOUNDED ON PRIVATE PROPERTY. IN THIS SYSTEM, WOMEN ARE SUBORDINATE . . ." I SEE. SO THIS IS HOW OUR SOCIETY EVOLVED . . .

New Lifers were desperate for any information, and secretly passed around banned books and scraps of paper about the outside world. Somewhere along the way, *The History of Social Evolution*,* written by a CCP member, was smuggled into the camp in small folios.

**The History of Social Evolution* was written by Cai Hesen, one of Mao Zedong's friends from his youth. Cai invokes Marxism and other Western theories to analyze the development of human civilization and criticizes traditional familial values, private ownership, and idolatry.

HEY THERE, SKINNYBONES!
ANG KING-SIONG.

LOOKS LIKE THE CABBAGES ARE DOING WELL.

SOME RECENT DEVELOPMENTS.

IT SEEMS LIKE YOUR NEW HEDGE IS REALLY WORKING.
YEAH! THE SEA WIND WAS TOO STRONG BEFORE. THE SODIUM WAS KILLING ALL THE CROPS.

YOU SURE ARE A HARD WORKER, SKINNYBONES! WHEN YOU FIRST VOLUNTEERED, I THOUGHT YOU WOULDN'T BE ABLE TO HANDLE THE WORK GIVEN HOW THIN YOU ARE—AND HOW YOU WENT TO HIGH SCHOOL AND ALL.

IT'S ALL THANKS TO YOU. YOU'RE THE ONE WHO TAUGHT ME ALL THE TECHNIQUES AND HELPED ME BUILD EXPERIENCE.

The soil and climate on Green Island were only suited to growing peanuts and sweet potatoes. In order to add more variety to the food, the squadron leader assigned Ang King-siong, an agricultural school graduate, to start a vegetable garden.
Khun-lim volunteered to be Ang's assistant, and together they managed to cultivate a wide range of leafy greens, fruits, and gourds.

KUN-LIN, I GOT MY HANDS ON THE LYRICS OF THAT "DANNY BOY" SONG.

REALLY? LET ME COPY THEM!

OW, IT HURTS!
TAI-LOK!
WHAT HAPPENED?
HE BEAT ME.
HE GOT ALL WORKED UP JUST 'CAUSE I WAS A LITTLE BIT LATE TO ROLL CALL TODAY.

While carefully applying Tiger Balm to the wounds, Khun-lim thought: *He's only seventeen, the same age as Khun-tsiong. To beat him like this for such a petty thing . . . it's heartless.*

Summer 1952. Liuma Channel.

IS YOUR SKIN BETTER?
NOT REALLY.
I THINK IT'S GETTING ITCHIER.

SHOULDN'T YOU GO TO THE INFIRMARY?
MM.

!

THAT'S YANG KUI!
HE'S BEEN JOGGING OUT HERE AFTER DINNER THESE DAYS.
EVEN A FAMOUS WRITER LIKE HIM IS BEING FORCED TO ENDURE HARD LABOR LIKE THIS . . .
LET'S GO, WE STILL HAVE TWO TRIPS!

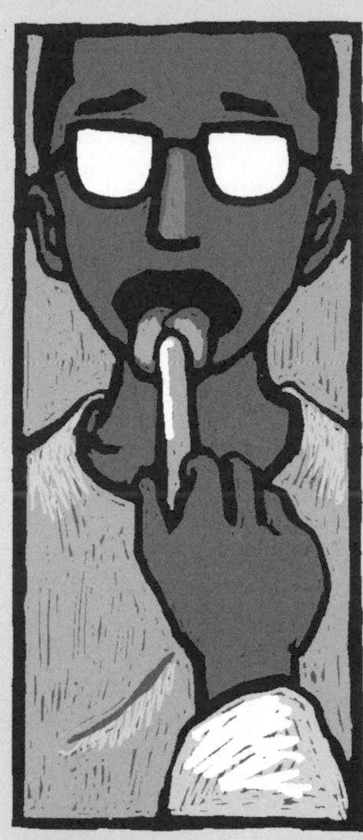

Dr. Lin En-kui
DIARRHEA?
A BIT.

In the 1950s, the Green Island New Life Correction Center had about ten practicing physicians, and an infirmary was established in the second year of the camp's founding. The doctors not only treated New Lifers, camp officers, and their dependents, but also the island's civilian residents.

IT REALLY ITCHES.

YOU HAVE PELLAGRA

PELLAGRA?

IT'S A SKIN DISEASE
THAT'S CAUSED BY NUTRIENT DEFICIENCY.
IT TENDS TO HAPPEN WHEN THE BODY LACKS
VITAMIN B AND PROTEIN AND IS GETTING
TOO MUCH SUN AT THE SAME TIME.

IT'S MOST COMMON IN
ORPHANAGES AND PRISONS. HERE,
I'LL GIVE YOU SOME VITAMIN B
AND OINTMENT.

TRY TO KEEP YOUR
SKIN COVERED
FROM THE SUN.
THANK YOU,
DR. LIN.
DR. LIN!
HIS HAND GOT HIT BY
A HAMMER!

AREN'T YOU HOT, SKINNYBONES?

HERE.

I'LL HEAD BACK FIRST.

OH, DANNY BOY, THE PIPES, THE PIPES ARE CALLING
FROM GLEN TO GLEN, AND DOWN THE MOUNTAINSIDE . . .

THE SUMMER'S GONE, AND ALL THE ROSES FALLING, 'TIS YOU, 'TIS YOU MUST GO AND I MUST BIDE . . .
HONG JIONG-SONG, WHAT ARE YOU READING?!
GIVE IT HERE!
IT'S JUST A LETTER FROM HOME!
STOP RIGHT THERE! STOP!
HAND IT OVER!
OH NO!
That day, Ang King-siong was put in the bunker. Khun-lim was anxious that he might have exacerbated Ang's sentence and also worried that he himself would be implicated. But the days passed, and nothing seemed to change.
Later, Ang was sent back to Taipei. He never returned to Squadron 3.

The bunker was built on the shore. It served as a lookout fort for soldiers but was also used as a confinement chamber for New Lifers. Being small and made of concrete, the bunker was extremely hot during the day and cold at night.

Autumn 1952.
As a preventative effort to curtail insurgence among New Lifers, the correction center decided to hold a special fete where New Lifers could arrange their own entertainment.
I CAN'T UNDERSTAND PEKING OPERA.
YEAH, AND IT'S SO FORMULAIC.
WHY CAN'T THEY JUST LET US GO REST?

I'D ALSO PREFER TO BE READING.

IT'S THE WOMEN'S SQUAD!
?
IT'S TSAI JUI-YUEH!

TSAI JUI-YUEH?
THE MODERN DANCER WHO TRAINED IN JAPAN? SHE WAS ALSO TAKEN PRISONER?
AH! I CAN'T BELIEVE THAT *THIS* IS WHERE I'M SEEING HER PERFORM FOR THE FIRST TIME . . .

Ah, how beautiful! Khun-lim was deeply moved by the performance.

He thought, *There are so many remarkable people here—Dr. Lin En-kui, the writer Yang Kui, the dancer Tsai Jui-yueh . . .* if they can *withstand this life, how can I complain about suffering as a twenty-something nobody?*

Lunar New Year, 1953. Khun-lim was twenty-three. It was his third year not being able to celebrate at home.

MOTHER IS THE MOON THAT SHINES ON OUR HOME
THE LIGHT OF PURITY, KINDNESS, AND LOVE

THAT SHINES ON THE WINDOWS, EVER-GENTLE
CLOUDLESS, AND NEVER LEAVES US WANTING

PRAISE AND HONOR HER: MOTHER, MOTHER.

I NEVER KNEW THAT THERE'S A JAPANESE VERSION.
I ONLY KNOW THE JAPANESE VERSION. WE SANG IT IN JUNIOR HIGH.
I ONLY KNOW THE CHINESE.
A CHINESE VERSION? WILL YOU TEACH ME?
MOTHER IS LIKE THE MOON SHINING DOWN ON OUR WINDOWS AND DOORS, PURE AND BENEVOLENT, THE LIGHT OF LOVE
MOTHER, I LOVE YOU, HOW GREAT YOU ARE, HOW I LOVE YOU

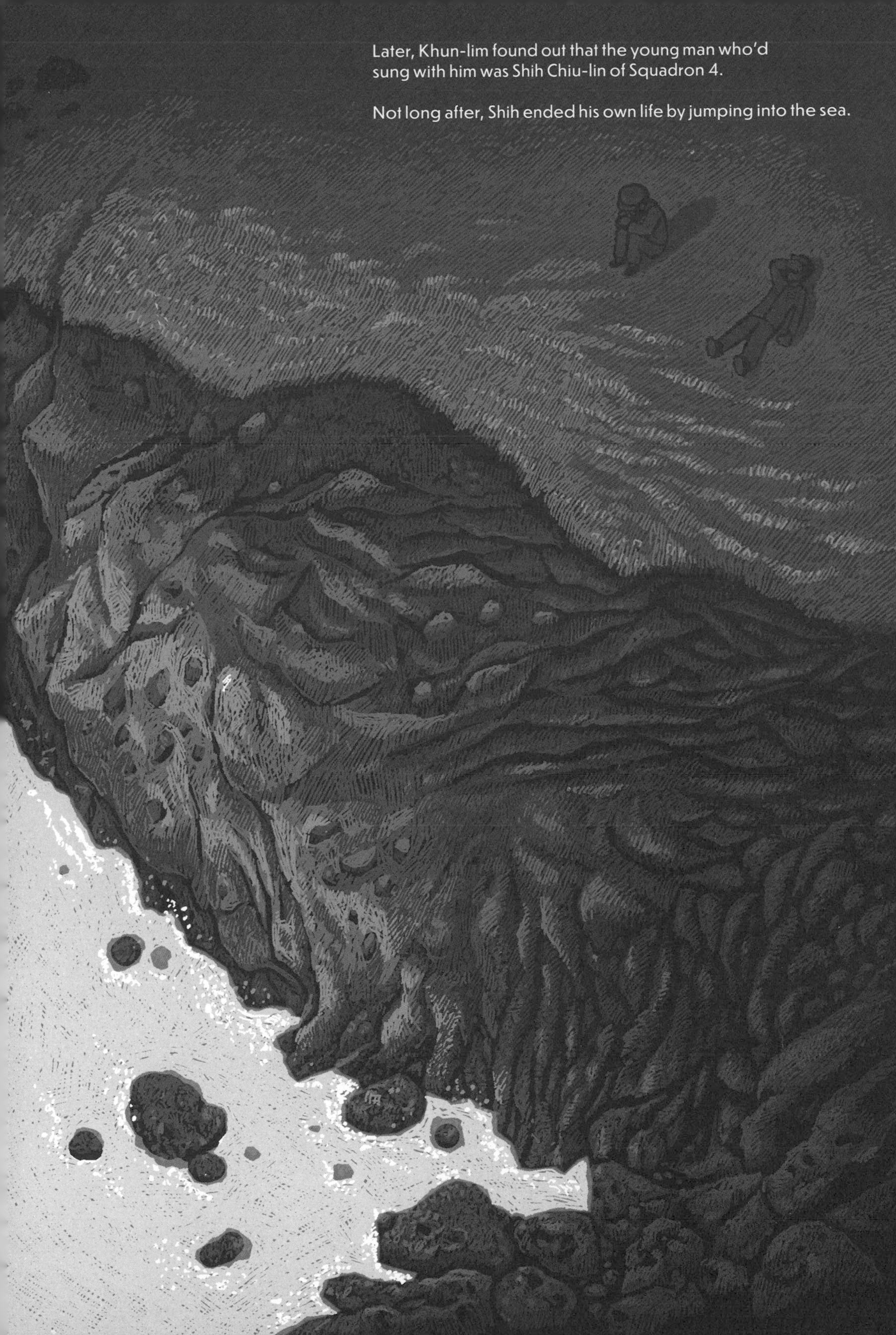
Later, Khun-lim found out that the young man who'd sung with him was Shih Chiu-lin of Squadron 4.
Not long after, Shih ended his own life by jumping into the sea.

WHOOSH!

YOU CAN DO IT,
TIUNN SIONG-BI!
?

PING-HONG, WHICH ONE'S TIUNN SIONG-BI?
THE ONE UP FRONT. THE ONE IN THE BACK IS NG TSHAI-BI.
YOU KNOW THEM?

YEAH, NG TSHAI-BI AND I ARE BOTH FROM TAINAN. SHE WENT TO TAINAN FIRST GIRLS' SCHOOL.

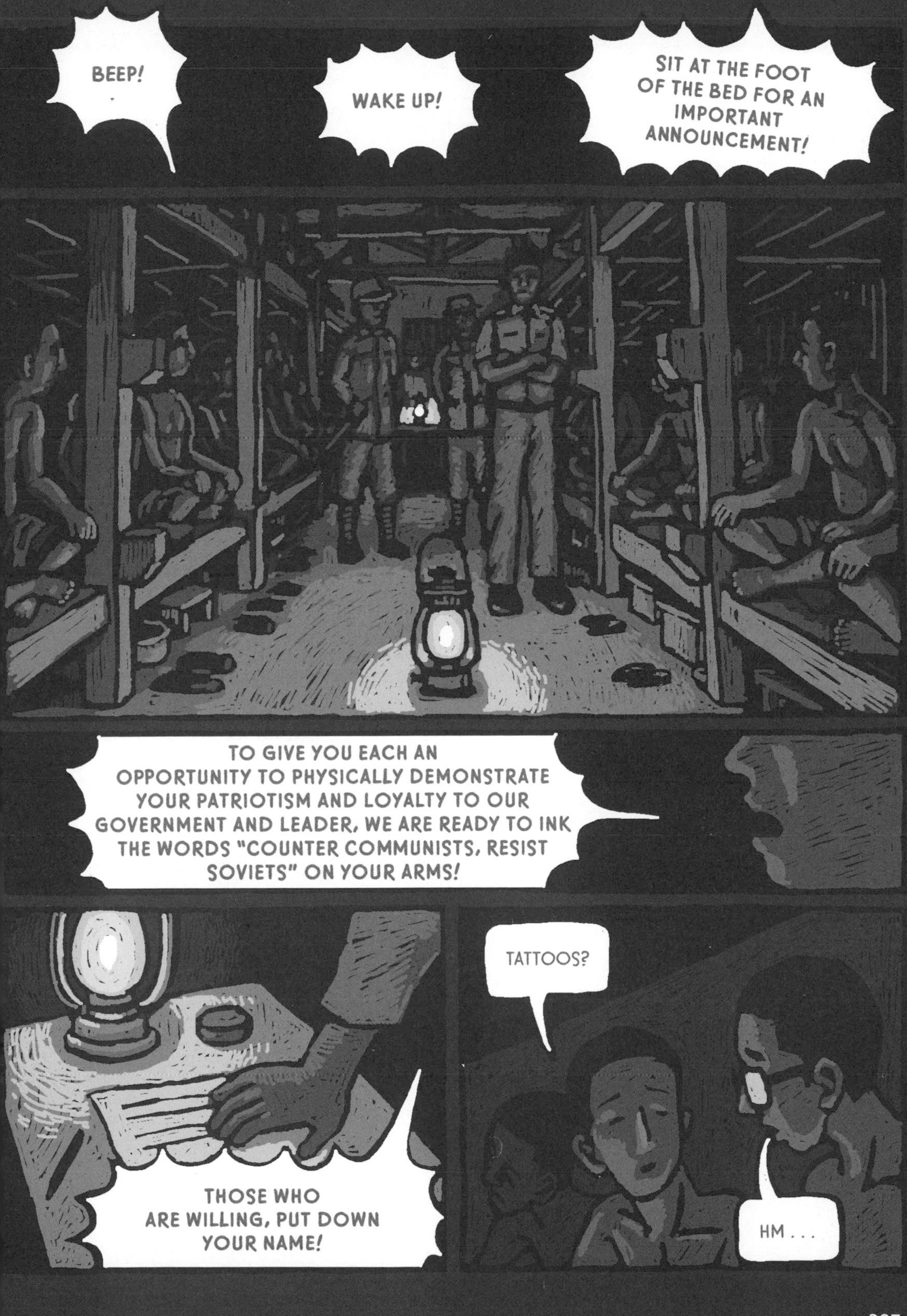

BEEP!

WAKE UP!

SIT AT THE FOOT OF THE BED FOR AN IMPORTANT ANNOUNCEMENT!

TO GIVE YOU EACH AN OPPORTUNITY TO PHYSICALLY DEMONSTRATE YOUR PATRIOTISM AND LOYALTY TO OUR GOVERNMENT AND LEADER, WE ARE READY TO INK THE WORDS "COUNTER COMMUNISTS, RESIST SOVIETS" ON YOUR ARMS!

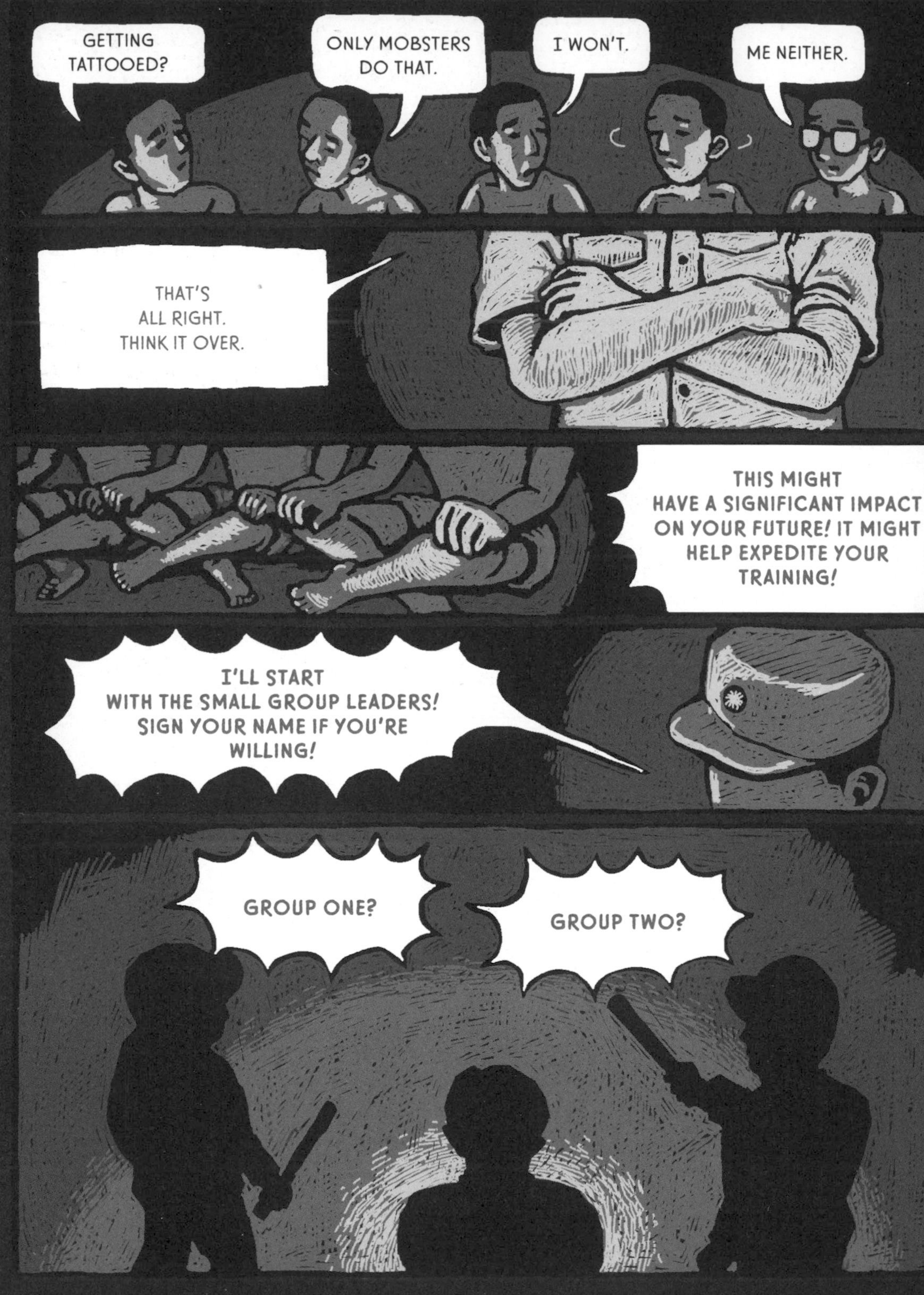
GETTING TATTOOED?
ONLY MOBSTERS DO THAT.
I WON'T.
ME NEITHER.
THAT'S ALL RIGHT. THINK IT OVER.
THIS MIGHT HAVE A SIGNIFICANT IMPACT ON YOUR FUTURE! IT MIGHT HELP EXPEDITE YOUR TRAINING!
I'LL START WITH THE SMALL GROUP LEADERS! SIGN YOUR NAME IF YOU'RE WILLING!
GROUP ONE?
GROUP TWO?

PERMISSION TO SPEAK!
CONFUCIUS TAUGHT US, "OUR BODIES, EVEN OUR HAIR AND SKIN, ARE GRANTED TO US BY OUR PARENTS; WE MUST NOT DAMAGE THEM; THUS BEGINS FILIAL PIETY." ARE WE NOT TAUGHT EVERY DAY TO HONOR SUCH TRADITIONAL CHINESE VALUES?
TATTOOS CLEARLY VIOLATE FILIAL PIETY. MIGHT WE DISCUSS THIS FURTHER?
... VERY WELL.
WE WILL LOOK INTO THE MATTER SOME MORE. DISMISSED! LIGHTS OUT!

March 1953. Among the Chinese POWs who surrendered in the Korean War and chose to be repatriated to Taiwan, many chose to get tattoos such as "Kill Zhu, Eradicate Mao" and "Counter Communists, Resist Soviets" to prove their loyalty. When news of this reached Green Island, the officers wished to adopt the same measure to please their superiors. However, New Lifers were unenthusiastic, which led the officers to strengthen their efforts at ideological control.

The following day.

BRING YOUR BELONGINGS OUTSIDE. NOW!

DUMP OUT YOUR KNAPSACKS!

ATTENTION! RETURN TO THE SLEEPING QUARTERS FOR HOUSEKEEPING!

!

TAN ING-THAI WAS ONLY SENT AWAY IN THE BEGINNING OF THE YEAR . . . I'M SO WORRIED.
YOU THINK THEY'RE PICKING ON OUR SQUADRON BECAUSE NOBODY VOLUNTEERED FOR A TATTOO?

ATTENTION!
THAT'S IT FOR TODAY!

TSAI BING-HONG!
HERE!

GET DRESSED AND REPORT TO ME.
YESSIR!

I WONDER WHAT IT'S ABOUT.

YOU'RE RESPONSIBLE AND HARDWORKING, PING-HONG. MAYBE HE WANTS YOU TO HELP WITH DESK WORK?

RUSTLE-
RUSTLE
WHOOSH

WHOOSH

RUSTLE

"SONG OF NEW LIFE."
5, 6, 7, 8!

THE SOUL OF THE CHINESE NATION HAS
ROUSED US FROM OUR DELIRIUM
THE THREE PRINCIPLES OF THE PEOPLE
HAVE CLEANSED OUR HEARTS
WE WILL REALIZE THE THREE PRINCIPLES
WE WILL SERVE LEADER CHIANG

RISE, COMRADES OF THE NEW LIFE
RISE, COMRADES OF THE NEW LIFE
UNITE AND STRIVE FOR EXCELLENCE
LET US BUILD OUR GREAT NATION*

YEAH, WEIRD . . .

WHERE'S TSHUA PING-HONG? IT'S ALMOST LIGHTS OUT . . .

*The squadrons had to sing "Song of New Life" during roll call.

Two days later.
KHUN-LIM!
NGOO TAI-LOK.

WHAT IS IT?
I GOT SOME ANSWERS.

THEY'VE PUT TSHUA PING-HONG IN THE BUNKER BY THE HILL.

WHY?
DID THEY FIND SOMETHING IN HIS KNAPSACK?

PROBABLY . . .
HE'S ONLY GETTING ONE BOWL OF RICE AND ONE BOWL OF WATER A DAY . . .

Tshua Ping-hong (Mandarin Chinese: Tsai Bing-hong) was interrogated over a letter he had sent to the young woman Ng Tshai-bi. Khun-lim agonized over the fact that he could not even bring water to a friend desperately in need.

Not long after, Ping-hong was taken back to Taiwan for a retrial.

I WONDER WHO'S COMING? THEY EVEN GAVE US NEW CLOTHES.
MUST BE SOMEONE HIGH UP.
FINALLY, NO MORE OF THOSE PISS-POT PANTS!*
THESE HAVE ZIPPERS!

GIN-SIONG, YOU LOOK GREAT IN THAT CAP.
HEHEH!

YOU LOOK LIKE YOU'RE DOING TAIWANESE OPERA!
WOO! GIN-SIONG THE CONQUEROR!

*So-called piss-pot pants were a type of simplified trousers where the waist opens into two pieces of fabric, which are folded and held up with a drawstring.

YOU SAW THROUGH US, KHUN-LIM!

THE TWO OF US ARE APPLYING TO PERFORM IN THE NEXT FETE.

DONG-DONG-DONG-DONG CLANG!

A few days later.

WHO COULD IT POSSIBLY BE?

THERE'S SO MUCH FANFARE.

WE'VE BEEN SWEEPING THE PLACE THREE TIMES A DAY!

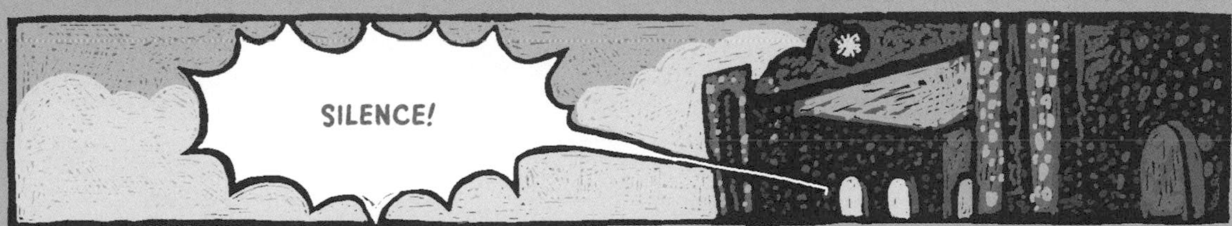

In April 1953, Wu K.C., whom Chiang Kai-shek had named Chairman of Taiwan Province, resigned from the KMT and escaped to the US with his wife. On February 9, 1954, he published articles in various newspapers refuting the ROC media's accusations of corruption. He also accused Taiwan's secret police of abusing their power and claimed that over 10,000 political prisoners were being held on Green Island.

The ROC government, to clarify that there were not so many prisoners on Green Island, invited journalists to visit the New Life Correction Center in April 1954. They were to be accompanied by Chiang Ching-kuo, Chiang Kai-shek's son and director of the political department, and Karl L. Rankin, US Ambassador to the ROC.

I HEARD THAT THE VIPS WHO CANCELED LAST TIME ARE COMING TODAY.
I CAN'T BELIEVE WE HAVE TO PUT UP SUCH A FRONT FOR THEM.
THEY'VE GONE AS FAR AS SENDING ALL THE RESISTANT COMRADES TO THE MOUNTAINS!
Khun-lim, who was working on the agricultural production team during the visit, did not attend the "festivities" nor act as a poster child for the foreign journalists and ambassador.

Chiang Kai-shek Hall.

NEW LIFER COMRADES!

YOU MUST ALL OBEY CAMP RULES AT ALL TIMES!

Director Zhou Wen-bin

THE PEOPLE SENT BACK TO TAIWAN LAST YEAR . . .

. . . AFTER FAILING TO FOLLOW ORDERS AND REFORM THEIR WAYS . . .

. . . HAVE ALL BEEN EXECUTED!

YOU MUST BE MINDFUL OF YOUR SPEECH AND ACTIONS, AND COOPERATE WITH US AT ALL TIMES!

DON'T TRY TO TEST THE BOUNDARIES OR SET AN EXAMPLE. IS THAT UNDERSTOOD?

ANG KING-SIONG?
TAN ING-THAI?
PING-
HONG . . .

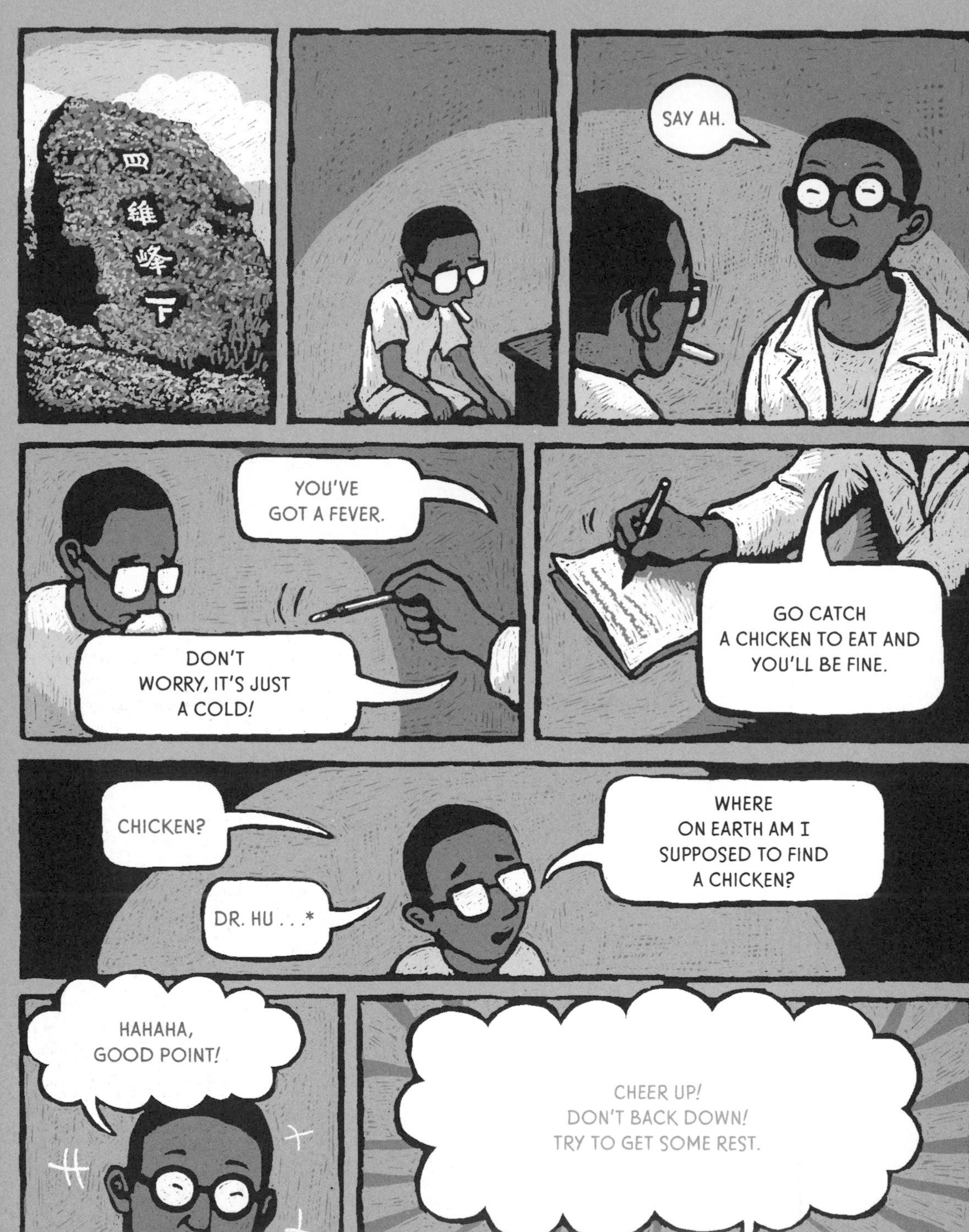

*Dr. Hu Hsin-lin was renowned for his wide-ranging knowledge.

Late February 1956.

FOR THIS MONTH'S CANTEEN COMMITTEE, TSAI KUN-LIN WILL CONTINUE TO DO THE SHOPPING.
PERMISSION TO SPEAK, SIR! I VOLUNTEER TO MAKE RICE INSTEAD!

!
?
!

YOU WEAR GLASSES, PLUS YOU'RE SO THIN— HOW CAN YOU MAKE RICE FOR EVERYONE?
IT'S RICE FOR MORE THAN A HUNDRED PEOPLE!
YOU'LL HAVE TO BOIL TWO LARGE VATS OF WATER. THAT'S OVER A HUNDRED KILOGRAMS!
PLEASE GIVE ME A CHANCE! I WANT TO GET STRONGER!

DON'T LET THE FIRE GO OUT. REMEMBER TO ADD COAL WHEN . . .

STIR THE RICE WITH THE SPADE

SO IT DOESN'T BURN.

HERE, YOU TRY.

MORNING!
MORNING!
TICK

During the month that he was in charge, Khun-lim never once burnt or undercooked the rice.

His true goal, however, was to stifle the pain of losing his friends by overwhelming himself with intense and continuous physical labor

October 1957. After dinner.

"HE FELT THAT THE MERIT OF HIS PAINTINGS WAS NOT EQUAL TO THE KINDNESS SHOWN TO HIM BY HIS BROTHER THEO. HIS WORK BEGAN TO SUFFER FROM AN INTENSE ADVERSE REACTION."

IT'S TRUE . . .
WITHOUT THEO'S SUPPORT, VAN GOGH WOULD HAVE BEEN TOO CONSUMED BY POVERTY TO MAKE ART . . .

Khun-lim thought of his younger brother, Khun-tsiong, who'd had to quit school due to Khun-lim's imprisonment. Nevertheless, Khun-tsiong still mailed over money and care packages every month.

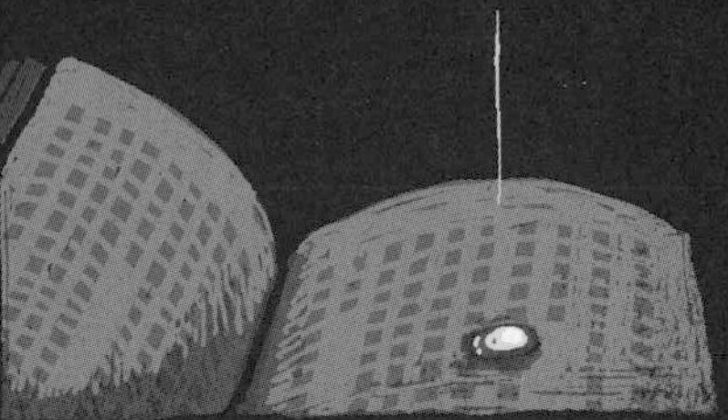

Book cover: *The Life of Van Gogh*

In addition to performing for each other, the New Lifers' Taiwanese opera troupe also performed on an open-air stage at the Green Island Elementary School during Lunar New Year. It became known as a major annual event by the island's civilian residents.

原子力発電の全て
英文字典
ANOTHER PACKAGE FROM YOUR FAMILY?
YEAH, MY ELDEST SISTER'S SON SENT A LETTER AND SOME BOOKS.
YOUR NEPHEW SURE IS DEVOTED TO YOU, SENDING ALL THESE BOOKS!
COME ON, LEND ME ONE.
YOU LIKE LOVE STORIES, RIGHT, TAI-LOK? THIS ONE'S PRETTY GOOD.
SURE.

Book cover: *Gone with the Wind*

I'm back on kitchen duty this month. Can you belie
that I can make rice for over a hundred people?
I, who couldn't even prepare a meal for myself back home! You know how much of a bookworm I was;
I barely knew how to do anything except to study.
Thinking back, I hardly went to the market at all.
Yet now it's been almost eight years since I left home.

How many "eight years" are there in a lifetime?
The idea of losing eight years must be an unimaginable horror to most people. At age twenty, I was almost paralyzed when I heard the sentence.
The prime of my life has drifted away
like passing water, never to return . . .

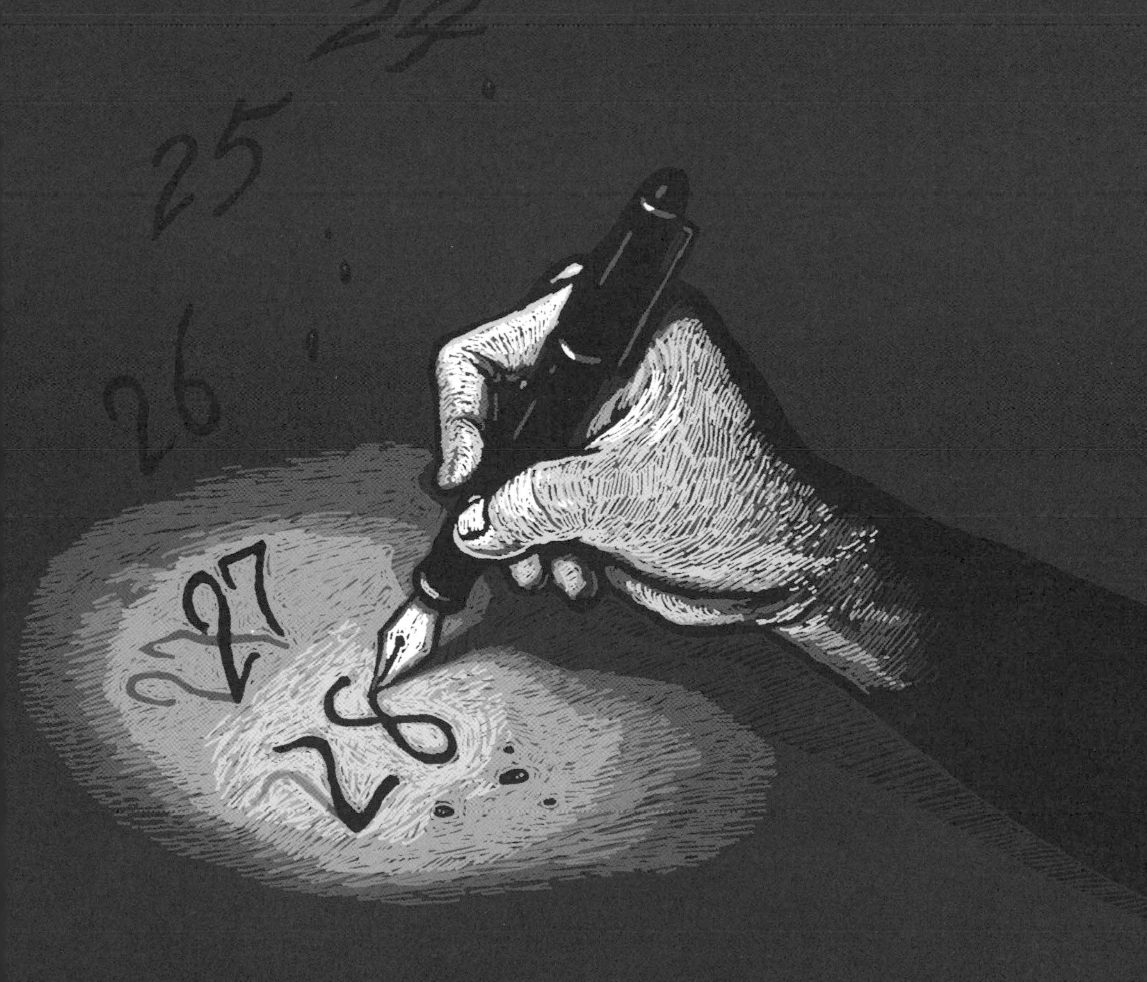

However, the passage of time has also allowed me to experience for myself what Ralph Waldo Emerson meant by this: a potted plant living in a greenhouse will never lack for sunlight, warmth, and care, but it will always be a mere plaything. For such a plant, an accident—the collapse of a wall or roof or a gardener's neglect—is an excellent opportunity. Its roots will dig deeper into the earth, its leaves will spread to cast shade, and it will benefit more people.

When a person meets with illness, injury, or bereavement, it feels at first like a blow from which they will never recover. But the truth is that, barring our human weaknesses, these misfortunes often prove to be revolutionary, pushing a person past the limitations of contented living toward a life of overcoming struggle, putting an end to childish ways of thinking, and creating a more mature, richer, deeper existence.

Lilies bloom all over Green Island in the early summer. Heading up the mountains, swinging a sickle, I sing at the top of my lungs into the blue skies, the great plains, and the vast seas below the steep cliff. In primitive times, labor and song were inextricably tied. While at work, I find myself in an untainted and affecting state of paradise.

Thank you for the books and shelving.
April 2, 1958

In 1959, Khun-lim was transferred from Squadron 3 to Squadron 5.

THIS PIGSTY IS SPOTLESS, MASTER SUI-TSUAN!
PIGS LIKE TO KEEP CLEAN.

WE'VE GOT TO KEEP THE PIGSTY CLEAN IN ORDER TO KEEP THE PIGS HEALTHY.

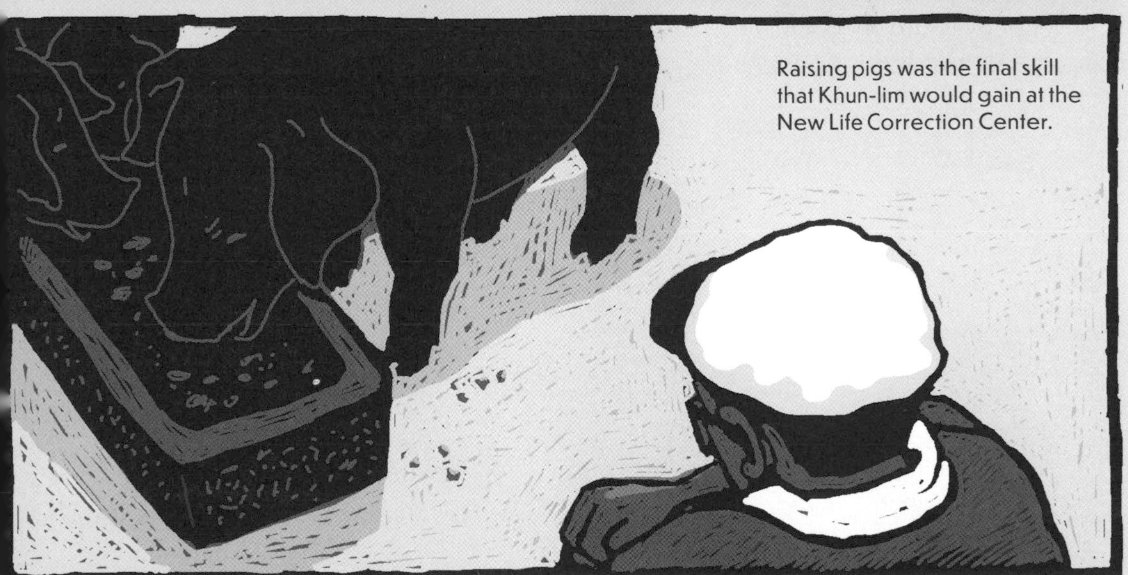
Raising pigs was the final skill that Khun-lim would gain at the New Life Correction Center.

台東縣綠島鄉流麻溝
蔡焜霖先生收

Dear Brother:
The whole family has been waiting for this day. At long last, you will soon return to us. We have prepared new clothes and shoes for you.

Sister's home isn't far from Taipei Main Station. It will be more convenient for you to exit from the Rear Station . . .
Love, Khun-tsiong

KHUN-LIM! COME HELP ME WITH MY HAIR!
COMING!

YOU GOT YOUR GUARANTEE SLIP?

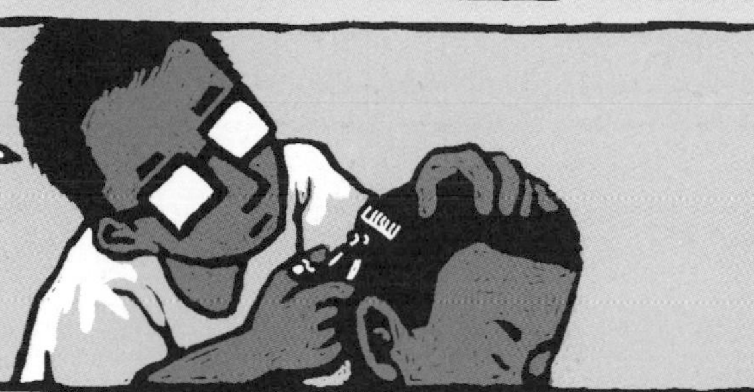
YEAH, MY SISTER'S HUSBAND AND HIS FRIEND ARE MY GUARANTORS.

MOST PEOPLE DON'T EVEN WANT TO BRUSH SHOULDERS WITH POLITICAL PRISONERS LIKE US, MUCH LESS ACT AS GUARANTORS! EVERYBODY'S AFRAID OF THE REPERCUSSIONS.
YOUR RELATIVES SURE ARE BRAVE!

AIGH, I SHOULDN'T SAY GOODBYE. I SHOULD SAY CONGRATULATIONS!
IF YOU GET OUT, NEVER LOOK BACK AGAIN.

BUT, WITH MY LIFE SENTENCE, WE REALLY WON'T SEE EACH OTHER AGAIN.
DON'T SAY THAT, MASTER SUI-TSUAN. WE'LL MEET AGAIN!

THANKS.
I WON'T DO YOUR HAIR, SINCE YOU'LL BE ABLE TO GROW IT OUT SOON.

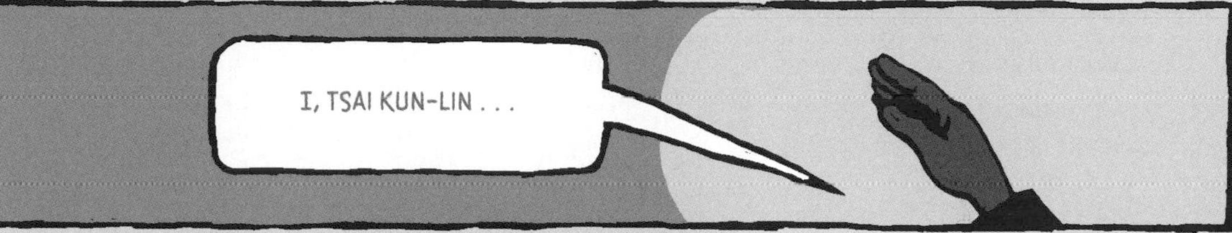

. . . AM GRATEFUL TO OUR BENEVOLENT GOVERNMENT FOR RELEASING ME TODAY. I HAVE LEFT BEHIND THE BANDIT COMMUNIST PARTY AND VOW TO WORK HARD IN SERVICE OF SOCIETY, BE LOYAL TO OUR LEADER, AND DEVOTE MYSELF TO THE REVOLUTION REALIZING THE THREE PRINCIPLES OF THE PEOPLE . . .
THEY TOOK AWAY MY PERSONAL FREEDOMS AND TEN YEARS OF MY YOUTH, AND NOW THEY EXPECT ME TO *THANK* THEM? WHAT A FARCE!

GOOD! YOUR REPORT CARD IS EXCELLENT. THE EXAM RESULTS SAY YOU'RE HUMBLE, PENITENT, AND EAGER TO BETTER AND CORRECT YOURSELF. TELL ME, WHAT ARE YOUR REFLECTIONS?
Director Tang Tang-ming

Boulder: Eradicate Communism, Restore Country

SIR, YES, SIR!
WHEN I FIRST ARRIVED, I COULD BARELY SPEAK CHINESE. BUT, AFTER MY EDUCATION HERE, I WON SECOND PLACE IN POETRY IN THE WRITING CONTEST.
MY LINGUISTIC TRAINING HERE WILL HELP ME CONTRIBUTE TO SOCIETY IN THE FUTURE.
FURTHERMORE, WHILE I USED TO BE SKIN AND BONES, I HAVE TRAINED TO GROW PHYSICALLY HEALTHIER AND STRONGER HERE ON GREEN ISLAND.
IN SHORT, I AM INFINITELY GRATEFUL TO THE CORRECTION CENTER, SIR!
VERY GOOD! WHEN YOU LEAVE, TAKE CARE TO MIND YOUR RESPONSIBILITIES AS A GOOD CITIZEN. DON'T ERR AGAIN IN YOUR THOUGHT OR BEHAVIOR.
YESSIR! THANK YOU, SIR!

革命之門

REMEMBER, DON'T TURN BACK!
MM!

I CAN'T TURN BACK.

THE SEA IS BEAUTIFUL IN LIFE AND IN DREAMS

LIKE YOUR VOICE IT TOUCHES MY HEART
THE ORANGE GARDEN HAS A FAINT FRAGRANCE

A SIGH FOR LOVE CUTS INTO MY HEART
HOW SAD THAT YOU WOULD LEAVE AND LEAVE ME ALL ALONE

I AWAIT YOUR RETURN IN THIS NOSTALGIC TOWN
COME BACK! ABANDON ME NOT

COME BACK! BACK TO SORRENTO

September 9, 1960. The day was clear and the sea calm. Khun-lim, having fulfilled his 10-year sentence, left Green Island on a fishing boat.

"Come Back to Sorrento." Lyrics: Giambattista De Curtis. Music: Ernesto De Curtis. A popular Neapolitan ballad written at the beginning of the 20th century.

South Link Highway.

Kaohsiung Train Station.

Sign under the flag: Taipei Rear Station

EXCUSE ME . . .

DOES MRS. TSAI CHIONG-TSI LIVE HERE?

MY MOTHER'S UPSTAIRS.

MY NIECE?
KHUN-LIM!
SISTER . . .
YOU WAIT
HERE, I'LL TAKE YOU
TO KHUN-TSAN'S!

Sign: Taipei Bridge

三重市農會
WE'RE HERE.
BA, MA, I'M HOME!
KHUN-LIM'S BACK!
BROTHER!

YOU'RE BACK, YOU'RE BACK . . .

WHERE'S BA?

BA!
BA!
WHERE IS HE?
WHY ISN'T HE HERE?

HOW IS THAT POSSIBLE?

TOOK HIS OWN LIFE?

WHY?

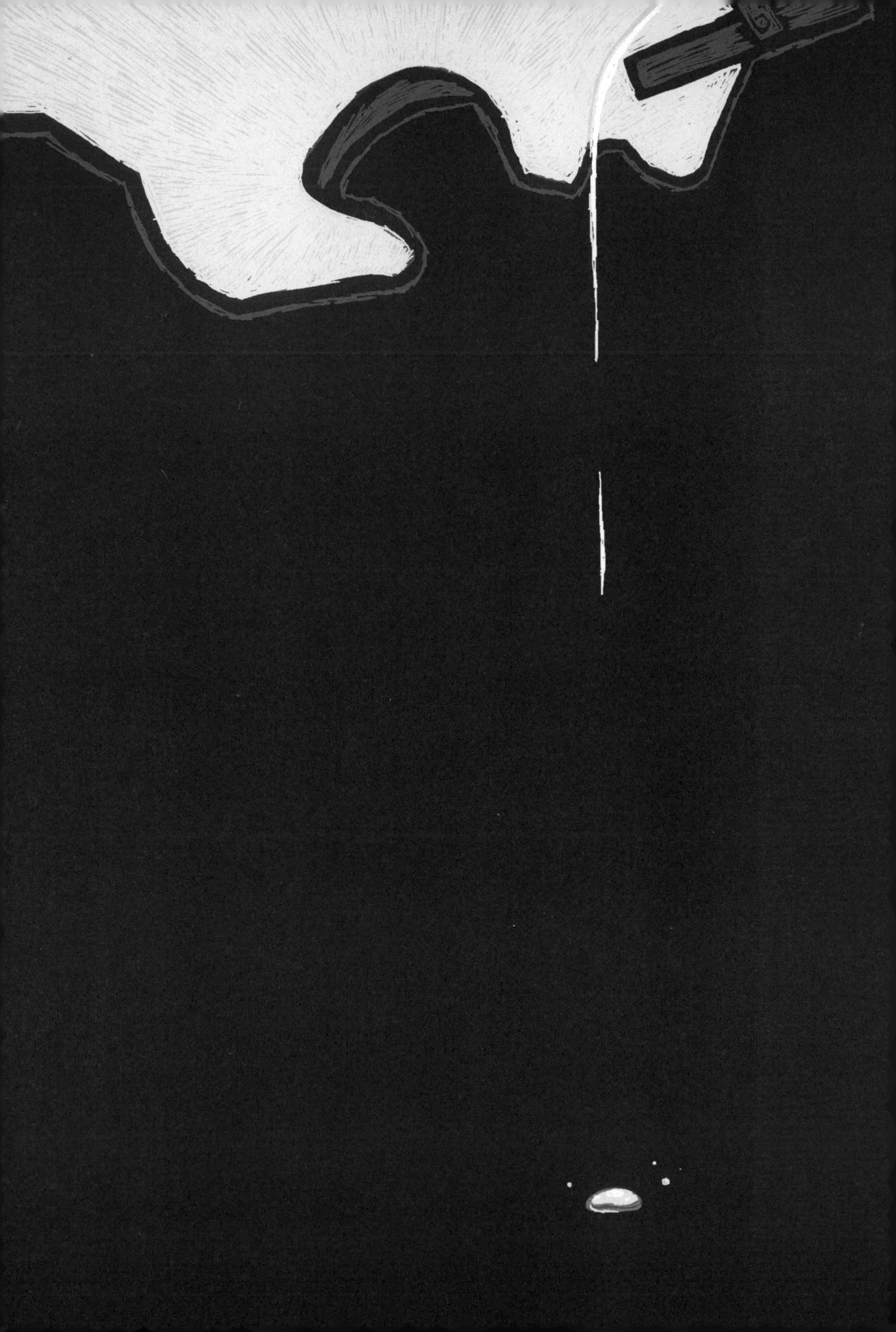

BA . . .
IT'S ALL . . .
MY FAULT . . .

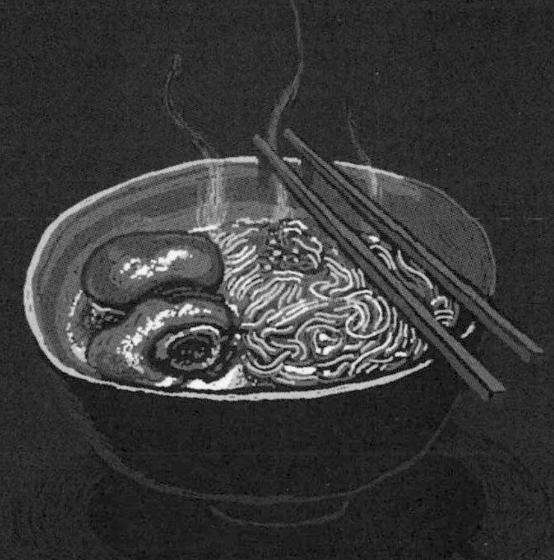
KHUN-LIM.
COME, DRY YOUR TEARS.
MA MADE BRAISED PIG'S FEET AND NOODLE SOUP FOR YOU . . . IT'S AUSPICIOUS; IT'LL TURN YOUR LUCK AROUND . . .

FURTHER READING

THE BOY FROM CLEARWATER
TIMELINE—PART 1

Year	K-L's Age	Events
1930	0	*December 18: Khun-lim is born as the eighth child to the Tshua family in Chingshui, Taichung (known under Japanese rule as Kiyomizu, Taichu).*
1935	5	*April 21: A major earthquake takes place in Chingshui. Khun-lim's family home collapses.* November 22: Under the Japanese, Taiwan holds its first local elections.
1936	6	*April 1: Khun-lim enrolls in kindergarten.* September: Taiwan's Japanese Governor-General launches the Japanization movement in Taiwan.
1937	7	*April 1: Khun-lim enrolls in elementary school.* July 7: The Lugou Bridge Incident takes place between China and Japan, and the Japanese Army occupies northeast China. The Second Sino-Japanese War begins. November 23: The Shinto shrine in Chingshui is completed.
1938	8	*Khun-lim falls in love with reading thanks to books by the Japanese publisher Kodansha.* May 5: Taiwan's Japanese Governor-General passes the National Mobilization Law, giving the government the right to manage distribution of manpower and resources during the war.
1939	9	September 1: Germany invades Poland. Three days later, Great Britain and France declare war on Germany. World War Two begins.
1940	10	June 27: Japan declares the "Japanese Monroe Doctrine," claiming that its invasion of Manchuria is founded on the aim to build a harmonious region where different East Asian peoples can coexist in peace. September 27: Germany and Italy formally accept Japan as one of the Axis powers.
1941	11	April 19: The "Japanization Guild" is established. December 6: Taiwan's elementary schools for both Taiwanese and Japanese children are renamed "national schools." December 7: Japan attacks Pearl Harbor. The US declares war on Japan. The Pacific War begins.

Year	K-L's Age	Events
1942	12	March: The so-called "Patriotic Volunteers of the High Mountain Tribes," composed of five hundred soldiers from Taiwan's indigenous communities, are dispatched to fight in the Philippines. June 4–June 7: The Battle of Midway takes place between the US and Japan.
1943	13	*April 1: Khun-lim enrolls in the junior division of Taichung First High School.*
1944	14	*Khun-lim and his classmates are forced to work at the military airport in Shuinan.*
1945	15	April: Khun-lim is enlisted as a student soldier. May 31: The US conducts an air raid on Taipei, killing over three thousand civilians. August 15: Japan surrenders unconditionally to the Allies. Taiwan is placed under the temporary control of the Republic of China (ROC). August 29: Chen Yi is appointed the Chief Executive and Garrison Commander of Taiwan. September 1: Japan enforces a military draft in Taiwan September: The Second Chinese Civil War begins. October 25: Japan signs its surrender letter to the Allies, represented by a general of the Kuomintang (KMT) in Taipei.
1946	16	*June: Khun-lim graduates from the junior division of Taichung First High School.* *August: Khun-lim partakes in the first annual Taiwan Province Youth Summer Camp.* *September: Khun-lim enrolls in the senior division of Taichung First High School.*
1947	17	February 28: The February 28 Incident results in civilian protests all over Taiwan. March 20: The KMT announces a "purge" to brutally suppress the uprisings. Khun-lim stays with his relatives up in the mountains to avoid the violence. April: Chen Yi resigns. Chiang Kai-shek restructures the government of Taiwan Province. May 15: Wei Tao-ming, the new governor, arrives in Taiwan. Wei declares an end to armed suppression. Classes resume.

Year	K-L's Age	Events
1948	18	*Khun-lim briefly joins a book club at school, reading leftist books of the 1930s.* May 10: "Temporary Provisions Effective During the Period of Communist Rebellion" are signed into effect by the KMT. Basic human rights are temporarily suspended.
1949	19	April 6: The KMT administration conducts large-scale arrests of student protestors for the first time during the April 6 Incident. The conflict heralds the White Terror period of the 1950s. May 20: Taiwan declares martial law. May 28: The "Political Traitors Punishment Law" passes and goes into effect on June 21, imposing capital punishment for treason, espionage, and defection. It is later regarded as one of the most inhumane laws of the White Terror era. June 15: Taiwan adopts the New Taiwan Dollar. *Khun-lim graduates from senior high and begins working at the Chingshui District Office. He passes the certification exam for teaching elementary school.* October 1: The People's Republic of China (PRC) is established. December 7: The ROC administration retreats to Taiwan.
1950	20	February 28: Chiang Kai-shek reinstates himself as president. June 18: Chen Yi, the former chief executive, is executed for espionage. June 25: The Korean War begins. *September 10: While working overtime at the Chingshui District Office, Khun-lim is seized by a plainclothes Changhua Military Police officer for questioning.*

THE BOY FROM CLEARWATER
TIMELINE—PART 2

Year	K-L's Age	Events
1950	20	February 28: Chiang Kai-shek reinstates himself as president. March 25: Chiang Ching-kuo, Chiang Kai-shek's son, is named Director of the Political Department, Ministry of Defense, as well as Director of the Presidential Intelligence Office, a predecessor to the National Security Bureau and the highest authority for political trials conducted during White Terror. Late April: Four leaders of the CCP's Taiwan Province Committee are arrested by the Secrecy Bureau. May 22: The US, being of the belief that the CCP will seize Taiwan, puts out an evacuation order. June 13: The "Statutes for the Detection and Eradication of Spies" are passed, establishing the legal basis for many arrests, interrogations, and convictions during White Terror. June 25: The Korean People's Army attacks South Korea, starting the Korean War. The following day, Chiang Kai-shek pledges to send troops in support of South Korea. June 27: US President Harry Truman orders the Seventh Fleet to assist Taiwan against the CCP. The US announces a policy to "neutralize" the Taiwan Strait. July 31: US General Douglas MacArthur visits Taiwan. One week later, Wu K.C., Chairman of the Taiwan Provincial Government popularly known as "Mr. Democracy," appears in *Time* magazine. Wu, who advocated for democratization, would go on to chafe more and more against the Chiang administration. *September 10: While working overtime at the Chingshui District Office, Khun-lim is forcibly seized by a plainclothes Changhua Military Police officer for questioning. He is later transferred to Tainan Military Police, Taiwan Provincial Security Command, Secrecy Bureau Southern Branch, and the Detention Center of the Military Law Office for the Taiwan Garrison Command.* October 8: The PRC deploys the People's Liberation Army to join the fighting in Korea, calling the Korean War the "war to resist the US and support Korea." *November: Khun-lim is sentenced to ten years of imprisonment for the crime of "joining a rebel organization and distributing flyers for traitors."*

Year	K-L's Age	Events
1951	21	*Early January: Khun-lim is transferred to Xindian Detention Center.* *March 10: Khun-lim's father, Tshua Mi-hong, visits him at Xindian Detention Center. This will be Khun-lim's last time seeing his father.* *May 17: Khun-lim is among the first group of political prisoners to be taken to the Green Island New Life Correction Center.* October: The US Congress passes the Mutual Security Act, launching an aid program that provides funds to different countries, one of which is the ROC.
1953	23	In the late spring, Green Island New Life correction center launches the "Every Man and Every Heart for the National Cause Movement," asking political prisoners to voluntarily get tattoos of slogans such as "Counter Communists, Resist Soviets." The movement is a failure, but the Correction Center officials accuse the prisoners of "renewed acts of rebellion" for "passively interfering with administrative affairs." Many prisoners are executed for this new crime. April: Chiang Ching-kuo visits the Green Island Correction Center. April 10: Wu K.C. resigns as Chairman of Taiwan Province. He and his family relocate to the US on May 24. July 27: The Chinese People's Volunteer Army, Korean People's Army, and the United Nations Command sign the Korean Armistice Agreement in Panmunjom, Korea. Fighting ceases in the Korean War.
1954	24	January 23: 14,207 Chinese prisoners of war taken during the Korean War volunteer to go to Taiwan. They become known as "Anti-Communist Martyrs," and the ROC later names January 23 "World Freedom Day" in their honor. February 9: Wu K.C. accuses Taiwan's secret police of abusing their power and claims in multiple newspapers that there are over 10,000 political prisoners held on Green Island. In April, Director of the Political Department Chiang Ching-kuo and US Ambassador Karl L. Rankin visit Green Island in an attempt to clarify that there are far fewer than 10,000 prisoners there. However, this inadvertently confirms the existence of the prisoner camps. December 3: The Sino–American Mutual Defense Treaty is signed in Washington, DC, by the US and ROC.
1958	28	August: The 1958 Taiwan Strait Crisis takes places, with the PRC shelling Taiwan's Kinmen Island. Tens of thousands of shells are fired in just two hours.

Year	K-L's Age	Events
1959	29	March 7: Chow Lien-hwa, a Baptist minister who served as chaplain to Chiang Kai-shek and his wife Soong Mei-ling, preaches on Green Island. Afterward, the camps relax their ideological regulations slightly, allowing prisoners to read the Bible and other apolitical books. August 7: Central and south Taiwan suffer from severe and widespread floods, affecting over 300,000 people.
1960	30	September 4: Lei Chen, director of the magazine *Free China*, is arrested for treason along with his colleagues. *September: Khun-lim completes his ten-year sentence and returns to Taiwan from Green Island.*

SOME NOTES ON THIS BOOK'S PRODUCTION

The art for the jacket and interiors was created by Zhou Jian-Xin using hand drawn illustrations in pink tones for part one and an infographics technique with a background color of light blue for part two. The text was set in Sequentialist BB, a comic book lettering font family inspired by crime noir, and the far-flung future as imagined in the 1950s. It has clean, legible lines and a deco feel. It was composed by Westchester Publishing Services in Danbury, CT. The book was printed on 120 gsm, FSC-certified paper and bound in India.

Production was supervised by Freesia Blizard
Book design by Andrea Miller
Edited by Arthur A. Levine and Arely Guzmán

LEVINE QUERIDO